HELLMANN'S
MAYONNAISE
Best Foods®

Over 100 Ways
— to —
BRING OUT THE BEST®

INTRODUCTION

Think "mayonnaise" and immediately salads and sandwiches come to mind. After all, what's a BLT or a classic potato or tuna salad without the mayo?

As changing lifestyles and eating preferences emerge, so have the uses of this versatile American staple. More than an essential salad and sandwich ingredient, mayonnaise can be used in a myriad of creative, convenient ways.

From sensational appetizers like Hot Artichoke Dip to enticing entrées like Magically Moist Chicken, mayonnaise is comfortably at home. Need dinner in a hurry? Let mayonnaise help you create a quick, tasty topping for micro-baked potatoes, or use it in a flavorful coating for grilled salmon steak. Even desserts and breads are delicious possibilities when mayonnaise is the unexpected ingredient in a moist carrot cake, rich microwave brownies or a wholesome banana-bran bread.

Keeping in step with today's calorie- and cholesterol-conscious consumers, all of the recipes in this book can also be prepared with light or cholesterol free reduced calorie mayonnaise with equally delicious results.

With this exciting collection of contemporary recipes, all carefully tested by our staff home economists, we invite you to discover the magic of mayonnaise. We're sure you'll find our seventy-eight year tradition of quality is still uncompromised!

Chicken Salad Supreme (page 26)

APPETIZERS

Smoked Salmon Spread

2 packages (3 ounces each)
    cream cheese, softened
3 ounces smoked salmon,
    finely chopped
1 tablespoon chopped fresh
    dill *or* 1 teaspoon dried
    dillweed

2 teaspoons lemon juice
1/4 teaspoon hot pepper sauce
1/4 cup HELLMANN'S® or BEST
    FOODS® Real, Light or
    Cholesterol Free Reduced
    Calorie Mayonnaise

In medium bowl beat cream cheese until smooth. Stir in smoked salmon, dill, lemon juice and hot pepper sauce until well mixed. Stir in mayonnaise until blended. Cover; chill. Spoon or pipe onto Belgian endive leaves or serve with party breads or crackers. Garnish as desired.

Makes about 1¼ cups

Southwest Chicken Fingers

2/3 cup HELLMANN'S® or BEST
    FOODS® Real, Light or
    Cholesterol Free Reduced
    Calorie Mayonnaise

1/3 cup prepared salsa
1½ pounds boneless skinless
    chicken breasts, cut into
    3 × 1-inch strips

In large bowl combine mayonnaise and salsa; set aside 6 tablespoons. Add chicken strips to mayonnaise mixture in large bowl; toss well. Let stand 30 minutes. Grill chicken 5 inches from heat, turning once, 4 minutes. Or broil, without turning, 5 inches from heat. Serve with reserved sauce.

Makes 6 to 8 appetizer servings

Smoked Salmon Spread

Spinach Dip

1 package (10 ounces) frozen
  chopped spinach, thawed
  and drained
1 1/2 cups sour cream
  1 cup HELLMANN'S® or BEST
  FOODS® Real, Light or
  Cholesterol Free Reduced
  Calorie Mayonnaise

1 package (1.4 ounces) Knorr
  vegetable soup and recipe
  mix
1 can (8 ounces) water
  chestnuts, drained and
  chopped (optional)
3 green onions, chopped

In medium bowl combine spinach, sour cream, mayonnaise,
soup mix, water chestnuts and green onions. Cover; chill. Serve
with fresh vegetables, crackers or chips. Garnish as desired.

Makes about 3 cups

Cucumber Dill Dip

1 package (8 ounces) light
  cream cheese, softened
1 cup HELLMANN'S® or BEST
  FOODS® Real, Light or
  Cholesterol Free Reduced
  Calorie Mayonnaise
2 medium cucumbers, peeled,
  seeded and chopped

2 tablespoons sliced green
  onions
1 tablespoon lemon juice
2 teaspoons snipped fresh dill
  or 1/2 teaspoon dried
  dillweed
1/2 teaspoon hot pepper sauce

In medium bowl beat cream cheese until smooth. Stir in
mayonnaise, cucumbers, green onions, lemon juice, dill and hot
pepper sauce. Cover; chill. Serve with fresh vegetables, crackers
or chips. Garnish as desired.

Makes about 2 1/2 cups

*Left to right: French Onion Dip (page 8),
Cucumber Dill Dip and Spinach Dip*

French Onion Dip

2 cups sour cream
1/2 cup HELLMANN'S® or BEST
  FOODS® Real, Light or
  Cholesterol Free Reduced
  Calorie Mayonnaise

1 package (1.9 ounces) Knorr
  French onion soup and
  recipe mix

In medium bowl combine sour cream, mayonnaise and soup mix.
Cover; chill. Serve with fresh vegetables or potato chips. Garnish
as desired. *Makes about 2 1/2 cups*

Maryland Crab Puffs

1/2 cup HELLMANN'S® or BEST
  FOODS® Real, Light or
  Cholesterol Free Reduced
  Calorie Mayonnaise,
  divided
9 slices white bread
1 1/2 cups (6 ounces) shredded
  Monterey Jack cheese

1 cup lump crabmeat or
  imitation crab, flaked
1/2 cup chopped green onions
1 tablespoon lemon juice
1/4 teaspoon hot pepper sauce

Lightly brush 36 miniature muffin pan cups with about 1
tablespoon of the mayonnaise. Trim crusts from bread; cut each
slice into 4 squares. Lightly press bread into muffin cups. In
medium bowl combine remaining mayonnaise, the cheese, crab,
green onions, lemon juice and hot pepper sauce. Spoon
1 heaping teaspoon crab mixture into each bread-lined muffin
cup. Bake in 350°F oven 15 to 20 minutes or until lightly browned.
(Can be made 1 day ahead. Cover; refrigerate. Reheat in 350°F
oven about 10 minutes.) *Makes 36 appetizers*

Crab Triangles: Instead of using muffin cups, lightly spread 1 side
of trimmed bread slices with about 2 tablespoons of the
mayonnaise. Place spread-side down on ungreased cookie sheet;
spread with crab mixture. Bake as above until lightly browned.
Cut each slice into 4 triangles.

Chilled Dilly-Tomato Soup

1 tablespoon Mazola corn oil
2 medium onions, chopped
1 clove garlic, sliced
2 pounds tomatoes (4 large),
   peeled, seeded and cubed
1/2 cup chicken broth
1 tablespoon chopped fresh
   dill *or* 1 teaspoon dried
   dillweed
1 teaspoon salt

1/8 teaspoon freshly ground
   pepper
1/2 cup HELLMANN'S® or BEST
   FOODS® Real, Light or
   Cholesterol Free Reduced
   Calorie Mayonnaise
1 tablespoon white wine
   vinegar
Tomato slices and dill sprigs
   for garnish (optional)

In 3-quart saucepan heat corn oil over medium heat. Add onions and garlic. Stirring occasionally, cook 2 minutes or until tender. Stir in tomatoes, chicken broth, dill, salt and pepper. Cover; simmer 10 minutes. Cool. In blender or food processor container place tomato mixture, half at a time. Process until smooth. Pour into large bowl. Stir in mayonnaise and vinegar until well blended. Cover; chill several hours or overnight. If desired, garnish with tomato slices and dill sprigs.

Makes about 5 cups

Hot Artichoke Dip

1/2 cup HELLMANN'S® or BEST
   FOODS® Real, Light or
   Cholesterol Free Reduced
   Calorie Mayonnaise
1/2 cup sour cream

1 can (14 ounces) artichoke
   hearts, drained and
   chopped
1/3 cup grated Parmesan cheese
1/8 teaspoon hot pepper sauce

In medium bowl combine mayonnaise, sour cream, artichoke hearts, Parmesan and hot pepper sauce. Spoon into small ovenproof dish. Bake in 350°F oven 30 minutes or until hot and bubbly. Serve with melba toast or corn chips.

Makes about 2 cups

Microwave Directions: Combine all ingredients in microwavable bowl. Microwave on HIGH (100%) 3 1/2 to 4 minutes, stirring once, until hot and bubbly.

Broiled Shrimp Chutney

1 pound medium shrimp,
  shelled and deveined
1/2 cup HELLMANN'S® or BEST
  FOODS® Real, Light or
  Cholesterol Free Reduced
  Calorie Mayonnaise,
  divided
1/2 teaspoon crushed dried red
  pepper

1/4 cup minced red onion
2 tablespoons chutney, finely
  chopped
1/2 teaspoon grated lime peel
2 tablespoons lime juice
1 teaspoon grated fresh ginger

In medium bowl toss shrimp with 1/4 cup of the mayonnaise and the dried red pepper. In shallow baking pan broil shrimp 5 inches from heat, turning once, 4 minutes or until pink. Cool slightly; chop finely. In medium bowl toss shrimp with remaining 1/4 cup mayonnaise, the onion, chutney, lime peel, lime juice and ginger. Cover; chill at least 1 hour. Serve on cucumber slices, rice crackers or wrapped in lettuce leaves. Garnish as desired.

Makes 1 1/2 cups

Green Onion Dip

1 cup HELLMANN'S® or BEST
  FOODS® Real, Light or
  Cholesterol Free Reduced
  Calorie Mayonnaise
1 cup sour cream

1/2 cup sliced green onions
1/2 cup parsley sprigs
1 teaspoon Dijon-style
  mustard
1 clove garlic, crushed

In blender or food processor container place mayonnaise, sour cream, green onions, parsley, mustard and garlic. Process until almost smooth. Cover; chill. Serve with fresh vegetables, crackers or chips.

Makes about 2 cups

Spring Herb Dip: Follow recipe for Green Onion Dip. Reduce green onions to 1/4 cup; omit garlic and add 1/2 cup dill sprigs.

Broiled Shrimp Chutney

Reuben Rolls

1/3 cup HELLMANN'S® or BEST FOODS® Real, Light or Cholesterol Free Reduced Calorie Mayonnaise
1 tablespoon Dijon-style mustard
1/2 teaspoon caraway seeds
1 cup (4 ounces) cooked corned beef, finely chopped

1 cup (4 ounces) shredded Swiss cheese
1 cup sauerkraut, rinsed, drained and patted dry with paper towels
1 package (10 ounces) refrigerated pizza crust dough

In medium bowl combine mayonnaise, mustard and caraway seeds. Add corned beef, cheese and sauerkraut; toss to blend well. Unroll dough onto large ungreased cookie sheet. Gently stretch to 14×12-inch rectangle. Cut dough lengthwise in half. Spoon half of the filling onto each piece, spreading to within 1 inch from edges. From long side, roll each jelly-roll style; pinch to seal edges. Arrange rolls, seam-side down, 3 inches apart. Bake in 425°F oven 10 minutes or until golden brown. Let stand 5 minutes. Cut into 1-inch slices.   *Makes about 30 appetizers*

Shrimp Louis Dip

1 cup HELLMANN'S® or BEST FOODS® Real, Light or Cholesterol Free Reduced Calorie Mayonnaise
1 cup sour cream
1/3 cup finely chopped green pepper
1/4 cup chili sauce

1 tablespoon prepared horseradish
1/4 teaspoon salt
1/8 teaspoon freshly ground black pepper
2 cups finely chopped cooked shrimp

In medium bowl combine mayonnaise, sour cream, green pepper, chili sauce, horseradish, salt and black pepper. Stir in shrimp. Cover; chill. Serve with crackers.

Makes about 3 1/2 cups

Reuben Rolls

Hot Cheddar-Bean Dip

1/2 cup HELLMANN'S® or BEST
   FOODS® Real, Light or
   Cholesterol Free Reduced
   Calorie Mayonnaise
1 can (16 ounces) pinto beans,
   drained and mashed

1 cup (4 ounces) shredded
   Cheddar cheese
1 can (4 ounces) chopped
   green chilies, undrained
1/4 teaspoon hot pepper sauce

In medium bowl combine mayonnaise, beans, cheese, chilies and
hot pepper sauce. Spoon into small ovenproof dish. Bake in
350°F oven 30 minutes or until hot and bubbly. Serve with corn
or tortilla chips. *Makes about 2½ cups*

Crab-Stuffed Mushrooms

1 package (6 ounces) frozen
   crabmeat, thawed and
   drained on paper towels
1/3 cup HELLMANN'S® or BEST
   FOODS® Real, Light or
   Cholesterol Free Reduced
   Calorie Mayonnaise

1/4 cup grated Parmesan cheese
1 tablespoon minced onion
2 teaspoons lemon juice
1/8 teaspoon hot pepper sauce
18 medium-size fresh
   mushrooms, stems
   removed

In small bowl combine crab, mayonnaise, Parmesan, onion,
lemon juice and hot pepper sauce. Broil mushroom caps,
rounded-side up, 4 inches from heat, 3 minutes. Remove and
drain well on paper towels. Fill mushroom caps with crab
mixture. Broil 2 to 3 minutes longer or until lightly browned.
Makes 18 appetizers

Ginger Lime Dip

1/2 cup HELLMANN'S® or BEST
   FOODS® Real, Light or
   Cholesterol Free Reduced
   Calorie Mayonnaise
1/2 cup sour cream

2 teaspoons grated lime peel
1 tablespoon lime juice
1 tablespoon honey
1 teaspoon minced candied or
   crystallized ginger

In medium bowl combine mayonnaise, sour cream, lime peel,
lime juice, honey and ginger. Cover; chill. Serve with fresh
fruit. *Makes about 1 cup*

Pesto Pizza

2 loaves (2 ounces each)
   regular size Sahara pita
   bread
1/2 cup HELLMANN'S® or BEST
   FOODS® Real, Light or
   Cholesterol Free Reduced
   Calorie Mayonnaise

1/2 cup grated Parmesan cheese
1/2 cup chopped fresh basil
1/4 cup pine nuts, toasted
1 small clove garlic, minced
   or pressed
   Fresh basil leaves for
   garnish (optional)

Cut each pita bread around edge, separating halves. Place cut-side up in shallow pan. Bake in 375°F oven, turning once, 8 minutes or until slightly crisp. In small bowl combine mayonnaise, Parmesan, basil, pine nuts and garlic until blended. Spread evenly on pitas. Bake 8 minutes or until puffed and lightly browned. Cut each into 8 wedges. If desired, garnish with basil leaves. *Makes 32 appetizers*

Winter Pesto Pizza: Follow recipe for Pesto Pizza. Omit fresh basil. Add 1/2 cup chopped fresh parsley and 1/2 teaspoon dried basil.

Chilled Zucchini-Basil Soup

2 cups chicken broth
3 medium zucchini, sliced
2 medium onions, chopped
1 tablespoon minced fresh
   basil *or* 1 teaspoon dried
   basil
1 clove garlic, sliced

1/2 cup HELLMANN'S® or BEST
   FOODS® Real, Light or
   Cholesterol Free Reduced
   Calorie Mayonnaise
2 tablespoons lemon juice
1/8 teaspoon hot pepper sauce

In 3-quart saucepan combine chicken broth, zucchini, onions, basil and garlic. Bring to boil over high heat. Reduce heat to low; cover and simmer 10 minutes or until zucchini is tender. Cool. In blender or food processor container place zucchini mixture, half at a time. Process until smooth. Pour into large bowl. Stir in mayonnaise, lemon juice and hot pepper sauce until well blended. Cover; chill several hours or overnight.

Makes about 4 cups

SALADS

Main-Dish Salads

Chicken Potato Salad Olé

2 large ripe tomatoes, seeded and chopped
3/4 cup chopped green onions
1/4 cup chopped fresh cilantro
1 to 2 tablespoons chopped, seeded, pickled jalapeño peppers
1 1/2 teaspoons salt, divided
1 cup HELLMANN'S® or BEST FOODS® Real, Light or Cholesterol Free Reduced Calorie Mayonnaise
3 tablespoons lime juice
1 teaspoon chili powder
1 teaspoon ground cumin
2 pounds small red potatoes, cooked and sliced 1/4 inch thick
2 cups shredded cooked chicken
1 large yellow or red bell pepper, diced
Lettuce leaves
Tortilla chips, lime slices, whole chili peppers and cilantro sprigs for garnish (optional)

In medium bowl combine tomatoes, green onions, chopped cilantro, jalapeño peppers and 1 teaspoon of the salt; set aside. In large bowl combine mayonnaise, lime juice, chili powder, cumin and remaining 1/2 teaspoon salt. Add potatoes, chicken, yellow bell pepper and half of the tomato mixture; toss to coat well. Cover; chill. To serve, spoon salad onto lettuce-lined platter. Spoon remaining tomato mixture over salad. If desired, garnish with tortilla chips, lime slices, whole chili peppers and cilantro sprigs. *Makes 6 servings*

Chicken Potato Salad Olé

Savory Orzo-Zucchini Boats

3 large zucchini
1/3 cup HELLMANN'S® or BEST
   FOODS® Real, Light or
   Cholesterol Free Reduced
   Calorie Mayonnaise
1/4 cup milk
1 tablespoon Dijon-style
   mustard
1 tablespoon lemon juice
1/4 teaspoon salt
1/4 teaspoon freshly ground
   pepper

1/4 teaspoon ground ginger
8 ounces cooked ham, cut
   into matchsticks
4 ounces Jarlsberg cheese, cut
   into matchsticks
2 cups coarsely chopped
   spinach leaves
2/3 cup orzo macaroni, cooked
   and drained
1/4 cup minced green onions

Cut zucchini lengthwise in half. Scoop out pulp, leaving 1/4-inch
thick shells; discard pulp. Cook shells in boiling water until
tender-crisp. Rinse with cold water; drain well. In large bowl
combine mayonnaise, milk, mustard, lemon juice, salt, pepper
and ginger. Stir in ham, cheese, spinach, macaroni and green
onions. Spoon into zucchini halves.   *Makes 6 servings*

Minted Lamb and Rice Salad

3/4 cup HELLMANN'S® or BEST
   FOODS® Real, Light or
   Cholesterol Free Reduced
   Calorie Mayonnaise
1/2 cup sliced green onions
1/4 cup chopped parsley
3 tablespoons minced fresh
   mint *or* 1 tablespoon
   dried mint
2 tablespoons lemon juice

2 tablespoons lowfat milk
1/2 teaspoon salt
1/8 teaspoon freshly ground
   pepper
1 cup uncooked rice, cooked
   and cooled
2 cups cubed cooked lamb
1 cup frozen peas, thawed
   and well drained

In large bowl combine mayonnaise, green onions, parsley, mint,
lemon juice, milk, salt and pepper. Stir in rice, lamb and peas.
Cover; chill.   *Makes about 6 servings*

Savory Orzo-Zucchini Boats

Pasta Salad Niçoise

1¼ cups HELLMANN'S® or
    BEST FOODS® Real, Light
    or Cholesterol Free
    Reduced Calorie
    Mayonnaise
2 tablespoons Dijon-style
    mustard
1 tablespoon chopped fresh
    tarragon *or* 1 teaspoon
    dried tarragon
½ teaspoon salt
⅛ teaspoon freshly ground
    pepper
2 cups small pasta shells,
    cooked, rinsed with cold
    water and drained

1 package (9 ounces) frozen
    cut green beans *or*
    1 pound cut fresh green
    beans, cooked and
    drained
1 can (6½ ounces) tuna,
    drained and flaked
¼ cup coarsely chopped red
    onion
    Assorted greens, cherry
    tomatoes and pitted ripe
    olives for garnish
    (optional)

In large bowl combine mayonnaise, mustard, tarragon, salt and
pepper. Stir in pasta, green beans, tuna and red onion. Cover;
chill at least 2 hours to blend flavors. If desired, garnish with
assorted greens, cherry tomatoes and pitted ripe olives.

Makes about 6 servings

Ham and Cheese Deli Salad

1 cup HELLMANN'S® or BEST
    FOODS® Real, Light or
    Cholesterol Free Reduced
    Calorie Mayonnaise
¼ cup red wine vinegar
1 tablespoon Dijon-style
    mustard
1 teaspoon salt
3 pounds potatoes, cooked,
    peeled and cubed

¼ pound cooked ham, cubed
4 ounces sharp Cheddar or
    Swiss cheese, cubed
½ cup chopped dill pickles
1 small red onion, chopped
3 tablespoons chopped
    parsley

In large bowl combine mayonnaise, vinegar, mustard and salt. Stir
in potatoes, ham, cheese, pickles, red onion and parsley. Cover;
chill.

Makes 6 to 8 servings

Pasta Salad Niçoise

20

California Fruit Salad

¹/₄ cup HELLMANN'S® or BEST FOODS® Real, Light or Cholesterol Free Reduced Calorie Mayonnaise
¹/₄ cup sour cream
1 tablespoon honey
1 teaspoon lime juice
¹/₂ teaspoon grated lime peel

2 cantaloupes, cut in half crosswise and seeded
4 cups assorted fresh fruit (strawberries, blueberries, honeydew melon and cantaloupe)
¹/₂ cup (2 ounces) crumbled blue cheese

In medium bowl combine mayonnaise, sour cream, honey, lime juice and lime peel. Cover; chill. To serve, fill each cantaloupe half with 1 cup mixed fresh fruit. Sprinkle each with 2 tablespoons blue cheese; top with 2 tablespoons dressing. Garnish as desired. *Makes 4 servings*

Oriental Salad

³/₄ cup HELLMANN'S® or BEST FOODS® Real, Light or Cholesterol Free Reduced Calorie Mayonnaise
2 tablespoons soy sauce
1 teaspoon sesame oil*
¹/₂ teaspoon minced fresh ginger
1 clove garlic, minced
¹/₈ teaspoon crushed dried red pepper
4 ounces linguine or thin Chinese noodles, cooked, rinsed with cold water and drained

1 cup cooked chicken strips
1 medium-size red bell pepper, cut into thin strips
1 medium cucumber, peeled, seeded and cut into thin strips
4 ounces snow peas
4 green onions, cut into thin strips

In large bowl combine mayonnaise, soy sauce, sesame oil, ginger, garlic and dried red pepper. Add linguine, chicken, red bell pepper, cucumber, snow peas and green onions; toss to coat well. Cover; chill. *Makes 4 to 6 servings*

*Sesame oil is available in the imported (Oriental) section of the supermarket or in specialty food shops.

California Fruit Salad

Turkey Waldorf Salad

²/₃ cup HELLMANN'S® or BEST
    FOODS® Real, Light or
    Cholesterol Free Reduced
    Calorie Mayonnaise
2 tablespoons lemon juice
¹/₂ teaspoon salt
¹/₄ teaspoon freshly ground
    pepper

2 cups diced cooked turkey or
    chicken
2 red apples, cored and diced
²/₃ cup sliced celery
¹/₂ cup chopped walnuts

In large bowl combine mayonnaise, lemon juice, salt and pepper.
Add turkey, apples and celery; toss to coat well. Cover; chill. Just
before serving, sprinkle with walnuts.

Makes about 4 to 6 servings

Shrimp Rémoulade

³/₄ cup HELLMANN'S® or BEST
    FOODS® Real, Light or
    Cholesterol Free Reduced
    Calorie Mayonnaise
2 tablespoons minced
    cornichons (midget sour
    gherkins)
1 tablespoon capers, well
    drained
1 tablespoon Dijon-style
    mustard

1 tablespoon chopped parsley
1 teaspoon anchovy paste
3 carrots, cut into matchsticks
1 medium celery root, peeled
    and cut into thin
    matchsticks
Lettuce leaves
1 pound medium shrimp,
    shelled, deveined, cooked
    and chilled

In large bowl combine mayonnaise, cornichons, capers, mustard,
parsley and anchovy paste. Stir in carrots and celery root. Cover;
chill. To serve, spoon carrot mixture in ring on lettuce-lined
serving platter. Arrange shrimp in center of ring.

Makes 4 to 6 servings

*Top to bottom: Country Cole Slaw (page 35) and
Turkey Waldorf Salad*

Antipasto Salad

1¼ cups HELLMANN'S® or
   BEST FOODS® Real, Light
   or Cholesterol Free
   Reduced Calorie
   Mayonnaise
⅓ cup grated Parmesan cheese
⅓ cup chopped parsley
¼ teaspoon dried oregano
¼ teaspoon dried basil
⅛ teaspoon freshly ground
   pepper
 1 clove garlic, minced or
   pressed

4 ounces thin spaghetti,
   cooked and drained
4 ounces salami, cut into
   matchsticks
1 can (14 ounces) artichoke
   hearts, drained and
   quartered
1 cup sliced fresh mushrooms
1 small zucchini, cut into
   matchsticks

In large bowl combine mayonnaise, Parmesan, parsley, oregano, basil, pepper and garlic. Stir in spaghetti, salami, artichoke hearts, mushrooms and zucchini. Cover; chill. Garnish as desired.   *Makes about 6 servings*

Chicken Salad Supreme

¼ cup HELLMANN'S® or BEST
   FOODS® Real, Light or
   Cholesterol Free Reduced
   Calorie Mayonnaise
¼ cup sour cream
1 teaspoon grated lemon peel
1 teaspoon lemon juice
½ teaspoon salt
⅛ teaspoon freshly ground
   pepper

3½ cups cubed cooked chicken
   breasts
½ cup sliced celery
¼ cup sliced green onions
¼ cup slivered almonds,
   toasted (optional)
   Assorted fresh fruit, cut up

In large bowl combine mayonnaise, sour cream, lemon peel, lemon juice, salt and pepper. Stir in chicken, celery and green onions. Cover; chill. If desired, garnish with almonds. Serve with assorted fresh fruit.   *Makes 4 to 6 servings*

Antipasto Salad

Steak, Bean and Potato Salad

1/2 cup HELLMANN'S® or BEST
  FOODS® Real, Light or
  Cholesterol Free Reduced
  Calorie Mayonnaise
1/2 cup milk
3 tablespoons prepared
  horseradish
1/2 teaspoon salt
1/4 teaspoon freshly ground
  pepper

1 pound small red potatoes,
  halved, cooked and
  cooled
  Romaine lettuce
3/4 pound cooked flank steak,
  thinly sliced
1/2 pound green beans, cooked
  tender-crisp
1 small red onion, sliced

In small bowl combine mayonnaise, milk, horseradish, salt and
pepper. In medium bowl combine potatoes and 1/3 cup of the
dressing; toss to coat well. On large lettuce-lined platter arrange
steak, beans, red onion and potato mixture. Serve with remaining
dressing.   *Makes 4 servings*

Dijon Asparagus Chicken Salad

1 cup HELLMANN'S® or BEST
  FOODS® Real, Light or
  Cholesterol Free Reduced
  Calorie Mayonnaise
2 tablespoons Dijon-style
  mustard
2 tablespoons lemon juice
1 teaspoon salt
1/2 teaspoon freshly ground
  black pepper
6 ounces tricolor twist or
  spiral pasta, cooked,
  rinsed with cold water
  and drained

1 pound boneless skinless
  chicken breasts, cooked
  and cubed
1 package (10 ounces) frozen
  asparagus spears, thawed
  and cut into 2-inch pieces
1 red pepper, cut into 1-inch
  squares

In large bowl combine mayonnaise, mustard, lemon juice, salt
and black pepper. Stir in pasta, chicken, asparagus and red
pepper. Cover; chill.   *Makes 6 servings*

Side-Dish Salads

Confetti Pasta Salad

1 cup HELLMANN'S® or BEST
    FOODS® Real, Light or
    Cholesterol Free Reduced
    Calorie Mayonnaise
3 tablespoons cider vinegar
2 tablespoons sugar
1 tablespoon milk
1 1/2 teaspoons dry mustard
1 teaspoon salt

8 ounces twist or spiral pasta,
    cooked, rinsed with cold
    water and drained
2 cups finely shredded red
    cabbage
1 cup coarsely shredded
    carrots
1 medium green pepper, cut
    into thin strips

In large bowl combine mayonnaise, vinegar, sugar, milk, dry
mustard and salt. Stir in pasta, cabbage, carrots and green
pepper. Cover; chill. *Makes 6 servings*

B.L.T. Potato Salad

2 hard-cooked eggs
1 cup HELLMANN'S® or BEST
    FOODS® Real, Light or
    Cholesterol Free Reduced
    Calorie Mayonnaise
1/4 cup sour cream
2 teaspoons vinegar
1/2 teaspoon prepared mustard
1/2 teaspoon dried Italian
    seasoning

1/4 teaspoon freshly ground
    pepper
3 medium potatoes, cooked,
    peeled and cubed
8 cherry tomatoes, halved
6 slices bacon, cooked and
    crumbled
1/2 cup chopped green onions
    Shredded lettuce

Separate egg yolks from whites. Chop whites; set aside. In large
bowl mash yolks with a fork. Stir in mayonnaise, sour cream,
vinegar, mustard, Italian seasoning and pepper. Add potatoes,
cherry tomatoes, bacon, green onions and egg whites; toss to
coat well. Cover; chill. To serve, spoon salad onto lettuce-lined
platter. *Makes 6 servings*

Easy Macaroni Salad

1 cup HELLMANN'S® or BEST
 FOODS® Real, Light or
 Cholesterol Free Reduced
 Calorie Mayonnaise
2 tablespoons vinegar
1 tablespoon prepared yellow
 mustard
1 teaspoon sugar
1 teaspoon salt

¼ teaspoon freshly ground
 black pepper
8 ounces elbow macaroni,
 cooked, rinsed with cold
 water and drained
1 cup sliced celery
1 cup chopped green or red
 bell pepper
¼ cup chopped onion

In large bowl combine mayonnaise, vinegar, mustard, sugar, salt
and black pepper. Add macaroni, celery, green pepper and
onion; toss to coat well. Cover; chill. Garnish as desired.

Makes about 8 servings

Note: If desired, stir in milk for a creamier salad.

Creamy Italian Pasta Salad

1 cup HELLMANN'S® or BEST
 FOODS® Real, Light or
 Cholesterol Free Reduced
 Calorie Mayonnaise
2 tablespoons red wine
 vinegar
1 clove garlic, minced
1 tablespoon chopped fresh
 basil *or* 1 teaspoon
 dried basil
1 teaspoon salt

¼ teaspoon freshly ground
 black pepper
1½ cups twist or spiral pasta,
 cooked, rinsed with cold
 water and drained
1 cup quartered cherry
 tomatoes
½ cup coarsely chopped green
 pepper
½ cup slivered pitted ripe
 olives

In large bowl combine mayonnaise, vinegar, garlic, basil, salt and
pepper. Stir in pasta, cherry tomatoes, green pepper and olives.
Cover; chill. *Makes about 6 servings*

*Top to bottom: Easy Macaroni Salad and
Creamy Italian Pasta Salad*

Ginger Fruit Salad

1/3 cup HELLMANN'S® or BEST
    FOODS® Real, Light or
    Cholesterol Free Reduced
    Calorie Mayonnaise
2 tablespoons orange juice
1/8 teaspoon ground ginger

2 medium oranges, sectioned
1 kiwifruit, peeled and sliced
1 cup fresh raspberries
    Sliced star fruit for garnish
    (optional)
    Pomegranate seeds for
    garnish (optional)

In medium bowl combine mayonnaise, orange juice and ginger.
Arrange orange sections, kiwi slices and raspberries on 4 serving
plates. Spoon dressing over fruit. Garnish with sliced star fruit
and seeds, if desired.   *Makes 4 servings*

Spinach Salad with a Twist

1 package (10 ounces) fresh
    spinach, washed, trimmed
    and torn
1/2 pound fresh mushrooms,
    sliced
7 ounces twist or spiral pasta,
    cooked, rinsed with cold
    water and drained
1 medium-size red onion,
    sliced
6 slices bacon, coarsely
    chopped

1 tablespoon Argo or
    Kingsford's corn starch
1 tablespoon sugar
1 teaspoon salt
1/2 teaspoon freshly ground
    pepper
1 cup HELLMANN'S® or BEST
    FOODS® Real, Light or
    Cholesterol Free Reduced
    Calorie Mayonnaise
1 cup water
1/3 cup cider vinegar

In large serving bowl combine spinach, mushrooms, pasta and
red onion. In medium skillet cook bacon over medium-high heat
until lightly browned. Remove with slotted spoon. Pour off all but
2 tablespoons drippings. In small bowl mix corn starch, sugar,
salt and pepper. With wire whisk stir into drippings in skillet
until smooth. Stir in mayonnaise until blended. Gradually stir in
water and vinegar. Stirring constantly, bring to boil over medium
heat and boil 1 minute. Pour over spinach salad. Add bacon; toss
to coat well. Serve immediately.   *Makes 8 to 10 servings*

Ginger Fruit Salad

Mediterranean Pasta Salad

1 cup HELLMANN'S® or BEST
  FOODS® Real, Light or
  Cholesterol Free Reduced
  Calorie Mayonnaise
1/3 cup milk
1/4 cup lemon juice
3/4 cup finely chopped fresh
  mint
1/2 cup finely chopped parsley
1/2 cup (2 ounces) crumbled
  feta cheese
1 teaspoon salt
1/2 teaspoon freshly ground
  pepper
7 ounces pasta curls or twists,
  cooked, rinsed with cold
  water and drained
2 medium tomatoes, seeded
  and chopped
1 medium cucumber, seeded
  and chopped
3 green onions, sliced
1 cup sliced pitted ripe olives

In large bowl combine mayonnaise, milk, lemon juice, mint,
parsley, feta cheese, salt and pepper. Add pasta, tomatoes,
cucumber, green onions and olives; toss to coat well. Cover; chill.
Makes 8 to 10 servings

Oriental Potato Salad

1 1/2 cups HELLMANN'S® or
  BEST FOODS® Real, Light
  or Cholesterol Free
  Reduced Calorie
  Mayonnaise
3 tablespoons vinegar
2 tablespoons sesame oil*
2 tablespoons soy sauce
2 teaspoons sugar
1 teaspoon grated fresh ginger
1/2 teaspoon salt
1/8 teaspoon hot pepper sauce
7 to 8 medium potatoes,
  peeled, cooked and sliced
1 1/2 cups diagonally sliced celery
1 can (8 ounces) sliced water
  chestnuts, drained
6 green onions, thinly sliced
  Lettuce leaves
2 tablespoons toasted sesame
  seeds

In large bowl combine mayonnaise, vinegar, sesame oil, soy
sauce, sugar, ginger, salt and hot pepper sauce. Add potatoes,
celery, water chestnuts and green onions; toss to coat well.
Cover; chill. To serve, spoon salad onto lettuce-lined platter.
Sprinkle with sesame seeds. *Makes 8 servings*

*Sesame oil is available in the imported (Oriental) section of the
supermarket or in specialty food shops.

Country Cole Slaw

1 cup HELLMANN'S® or BEST
  FOODS® Real, Light or
  Cholesterol Free Reduced
  Calorie Mayonnaise
3 tablespoons lemon juice
2 tablespoons sugar

1 teaspoon salt
6 cups shredded cabbage
1 cup shredded carrots
1/2 cup chopped or thinly
  sliced green pepper

In medium bowl combine mayonnaise, lemon juice, sugar and
salt. Stir in cabbage, carrots and green pepper. Cover; chill.

Makes about 10 servings

Vegetable Rice Salad

1 cup HELLMANN'S® or BEST
  FOODS® Real, Light or
  Cholesterol Free Reduced
  Calorie Mayonnaise
1 tablespoon vinegar
1 small clove garlic, minced
1 teaspoon salt

1/4 teaspoon freshly ground
  pepper
2 cups cooked rice, cooled
1 package (10 ounces) frozen
  peas, thawed and drained
1/2 cup shredded carrot
1/4 cup chopped green onions

In medium bowl combine mayonnaise, vinegar, garlic, salt and
pepper. Add rice, peas, carrot and green onions; toss to coat well.
Cover; chill.

Makes about 6 servings

Classic Waldorf Salad

1/2 cup HELLMANN'S® or BEST
  FOODS® Real, Light or
  Cholesterol Free Reduced
  Calorie Mayonnaise
1 tablespoon sugar
1 tablespoon lemon juice

1/8 teaspoon salt
3 medium-size red apples,
  cored and diced
1 cup sliced celery
1/2 cup chopped walnuts

In medium bowl combine mayonnaise, sugar, lemon juice and
salt. Add apples and celery; toss to coat well. Cover; chill. Just
before serving, sprinkle with walnuts.

Makes about 8 servings

Dijon Potato Salad

1 cup HELLMANN'S® or BEST FOODS® Real, Light or Cholesterol Free Reduced Calorie Mayonnaise
2 tablespoons Dijon-style mustard
2 tablespoons chopped fresh dill *or* 1 1/2 teaspoons dried dillweed
1/2 teaspoon salt
1/4 teaspoon freshly ground pepper
1 1/2 pounds small red potatoes, cooked and quartered
1 cup sliced radishes
1/2 cup chopped green onions

In large bowl combine mayonnaise, mustard, dill, salt and pepper. Stir in potatoes, radishes and green onions. Cover; chill.

Makes about 8 servings

Classic Potato Salad

1 cup HELLMANN'S® or BEST FOODS® Real, Light or Cholesterol Free Reduced Calorie Mayonnaise
2 tablespoons vinegar
1 1/2 teaspoons salt
1 teaspoon sugar
1/4 teaspoon freshly ground pepper
5 to 6 medium potatoes, peeled, cooked and cubed
1 cup sliced celery
1/2 cup chopped onion
2 hard-cooked eggs, chopped

In large bowl combine mayonnaise, vinegar, salt, sugar and pepper. Add potatoes, celery, onion and eggs; toss to coat well. Cover; chill.

Makes about 8 servings

Top to bottom: Dijon Potato Salad and Classic Potato Salad

Southwest Ruffle Salad

2/3 cup HELLMANN'S® or BEST FOODS® Real, Light or Cholesterol Free Reduced Calorie Mayonnaise
1/3 cup sour cream
1/4 cup chopped fresh cilantro
2 tablespoons milk
2 tablespoons lime juice
1 fresh jalapeño pepper, seeded and minced*
1 teaspoon salt
7 ounces pasta ruffles or radiatore, cooked, rinsed with cold water and drained

2 large tomatoes, seeded and chopped
1 yellow bell pepper, cut into matchsticks
1 zucchini, quartered lengthwise and thinly sliced
3 green onions, thinly sliced

In large bowl combine mayonnaise, sour cream, cilantro, milk, lime juice, jalapeño pepper and salt. Add pasta, tomatoes, yellow bell pepper, zucchini and green onions; toss to coat well. Cover; chill.   *Makes 6 to 8 servings*

*Wear rubber gloves when working with hot peppers and wash hands in warm soapy water. Avoid touching face or eyes.

Crunchy Potato Chip Salad

1 cup HELLMANN'S® or BEST FOODS® Real, Light or Cholesterol Free Reduced Calorie Mayonnaise
2 tablespoons vinegar
2 cups finely shredded cabbage

1 can (6 1/2 ounces) tuna, drained and flaked
1/3 cup shredded carrot
1/3 cup chopped green pepper
2 tablespoons minced onion
2 1/2 cups potato chips

In medium bowl combine mayonnaise and vinegar. Stir in cabbage, tuna, carrot, green pepper and onion. Cover; chill. *Just before serving*, add potato chips; toss lightly.

Makes 6 servings

Southwest Ruffle Salad

Sweet Potato Salad

2 pounds sweet potatoes,
  peeled and cubed
2 tablespoons lemon juice
1 cup HELLMANN'S® or BEST
  FOODS® Real, Light or
  Cholesterol Free Reduced
  Calorie Mayonnaise
1 teaspoon grated orange peel
2 tablespoons orange juice
1 tablespoon honey
1 teaspoon chopped fresh
  ginger

¹/₄ teaspoon salt
¹/₈ teaspoon nutmeg
1 cup coarsely chopped
  pecans
1 cup sliced celery
¹/₃ cup chopped pitted dates
  Lettuce leaves
1 can (11 ounces) mandarin
  orange sections, drained

In medium saucepan cook potatoes 8 to 10 minutes in boiling, salted water just until tender. (Do not overcook.) Drain. Toss with lemon juice. In large bowl combine mayonnaise, orange peel, orange juice, honey, ginger, salt and nutmeg. Stir in warm potatoes, pecans, celery and dates. Cover; chill. To serve, spoon salad onto lettuce-lined platter. Arrange orange sections around salad. Garnish as desired.   *Makes 6 servings*

Greek Summer Salad

1 cup HELLMANN'S® or BEST
  FOODS® Real, Light or
  Cholesterol Free Reduced
  Calorie Mayonnaise
¹/₂ cup plain yogurt
1 tablespoon chopped fresh
  mint *or* 1 teaspoon
  dried mint
1 medium clove garlic,
  minced

1 teaspoon salt, or to taste
¹/₈ teaspoon freshly ground
  pepper
1¹/₂ pounds small red potatoes,
  cooked and cubed
2 medium cucumbers, peeled,
  seeded and cubed
¹/₂ cup chopped green onions
  Fresh mint for garnish
  (optional)

In large bowl combine mayonnaise, yogurt, mint, garlic, salt and pepper. Add potatoes, cucumbers and green onions; toss to coat well. Cover; chill. To serve, turn into serving bowl and garnish with mint.   *Makes 8 servings*

Sweet Potato Salad

Tuna Salad Positano

1 1/2 cups HELLMANN'S® or
BEST FOODS® Real, Light
or Cholesterol Free
Reduced Calorie
Mayonnaise
1 can (6 1/2 ounces) tuna,
drained
6 anchovies
3 tablespoons capers, drained,
divided

2 tablespoons lemon juice
8 ounces elbow macaroni,
cooked, rinsed with cold
water and drained
2 cups broccoli florets,
cooked tender-crisp
1 cup sliced carrots, cooked
tender-crisp

In blender or food processor container combine mayonnaise,
tuna, anchovies, 1 tablespoon of the capers and the lemon juice;
process until smooth. Stir in remaining 2 tablespoons capers. In
large bowl combine macaroni, broccoli and carrots. Add dressing;
toss to coat well.   *Makes 6 to 8 servings*

Potato Salad Italian-Style

1 1/2 cups HELLMANN'S® or
BEST FOODS® Real, Light
or Cholesterol Free
Reduced Calorie
Mayonnaise
1/4 cup Mazola corn oil
2 tablespoons wine vinegar
1 tablespoon chopped fresh
basil *or* 1 teaspoon
dried basil
1 1/2 teaspoons chopped fresh
oregano *or* 1/2 teaspoon
dried oregano
1 clove garlic, minced
1/2 teaspoon freshly ground
black pepper

3 pounds small red potatoes,
cooked and quartered
1 jar (7 1/4 ounces) roasted red
peppers, drained and cut
into 1/2-inch strips
1 jar (6 ounces) marinated
artichoke hearts, drained
and quartered
1 can (6 ounces) pitted ripe
olives, drained and cut in
half
1 cup thinly sliced pepperoni
Salt to taste

In large bowl combine mayonnaise, corn oil, vinegar, basil,
oregano, garlic and black pepper. Add potatoes, roasted red
peppers, artichoke hearts, olives, pepperoni and salt to taste; toss
to coat well. Serve at room temperature or cover and chill.
Makes 8 servings

Salad Dressings

Creamy Onion Dressing

1 cup HELLMANN'S® or BEST
    FOODS® Real, Light or
    Cholesterol Free Reduced
    Calorie Mayonnaise
1 tablespoon cider vinegar

1 tablespoon milk
1 tablespoon grated onion
1/2 teaspoon sugar
1/4 teaspoon salt

In small bowl combine mayonnaise, vinegar, milk, onion, sugar and salt. Cover; chill. *Makes about 1 cup*

Creamy Garlic Dressing: Follow recipe for Creamy Onion Dressing. Omit onion. Add 1 medium clove garlic, minced or pressed.

Louis Dressing

1 cup HELLMANN'S® or BEST
    FOODS® Real, Light or
    Cholesterol Free Reduced
    Calorie Mayonnaise
1/2 cup chili sauce
1 tablespoon minced parsley
1 teaspoon lemon juice

1 teaspoon prepared
    horseradish
1/2 teaspoon grated onion
1/8 teaspoon salt
1/8 teaspoon freshly ground
    pepper

In small bowl combine mayonnaise, chili sauce, parsley, lemon juice, horseradish, onion, salt and pepper. Cover; chill.

Makes 1 1/2 cups

Creamy French Dressing

1 cup HELLMANN'S® or BEST
   FOODS® Real, Light or
   Cholesterol Free Reduced
   Calorie Mayonnaise
2 tablespoons lemon juice or
   vinegar
4 teaspoons sugar

1 tablespoon milk
1 teaspoon paprika
$1/2$ teaspoon dry mustard
$1/4$ teaspoon salt
$1/8$ teaspoon freshly ground
   pepper

In small bowl combine mayonnaise, lemon juice, sugar, milk, paprika, dry mustard, salt and pepper. Cover; chill.

Makes about 1$1/4$ cups

Chunky Blue Cheese Dressing

1 cup HELLMANN'S® or BEST
   FOODS® Real, Light or
   Cholesterol Free Reduced
   Calorie Mayonnaise
$1/2$ cup (2 ounces) crumbled
   blue cheese

2 tablespoons milk
2 tablespoons cider vinegar
2 teaspoons sugar
$1/4$ teaspoon onion salt
$1/4$ teaspoon dry mustard
$1/8$ teaspoon garlic powder

In small bowl combine mayonnaise, cheese, milk, vinegar, sugar, onion salt, dry mustard and garlic powder. Cover; chill.

Makes about 1$1/2$ cups

Note: For best results, use Real Mayonnaise. If using Light or Cholesterol Free Reduced Calorie Mayonnaise, use dressing the same day.

Clockwise from left: Creamy French Dressing,
Chunky Blue Cheese Dressing and
Creamy Italian Dressing (page 46)

Creamy Italian Dressing

1 cup HELLMANN'S® or BEST
  FOODS® Real, Light or
  Cholesterol Free Reduced
  Calorie Mayonnaise
1/2 small onion
2 tablespoons red wine
  vinegar
1 tablespoon sugar

3/4 teaspoon dried Italian
  seasoning
1/4 teaspoon salt
1/4 teaspoon garlic salt or
  powder
1/8 teaspoon freshly ground
  pepper

In blender or food processor container combine mayonnaise,
onion, vinegar, sugar, Italian seasoning, salt, garlic salt and
pepper. Process until smooth. Cover; chill. *Makes 1¼ cups*

Thousand Island Dressing

1 cup HELLMANN'S® or BEST
  FOODS® Real, Light or
  Cholesterol Free Reduced
  Calorie Mayonnaise
1/3 cup chili sauce or ketchup

1/4 cup sweet pickle relish
1 tablespoon chopped onion
1 hard-cooked egg, chopped
  (optional)

In small bowl combine mayonnaise, chili sauce, pickle relish,
onion and egg. Cover; chill. *Makes 2 cups*

Russian Dressing

1 cup HELLMANN'S® or BEST
  FOODS® Real, Light or
  Cholesterol Free Reduced
  Calorie Mayonnaise
1/3 cup chili sauce or ketchup

1/3 cup chopped drained
  pickles
2 teaspoons lemon juice
2 teaspoons sugar

In small bowl combine mayonnaise, chili sauce, pickles, lemon
juice and sugar. Cover; chill. *Makes about 1½ cups*

Cole Slaw Dressing

1 cup HELLMANN'S® or BEST
   FOODS® Real, Light or
   Cholesterol Free Reduced
   Calorie Mayonnaise
3 tablespoons sugar

3 tablespoons cider vinegar
1 tablespoon milk
1 teaspoon salt
1/4 teaspoon dry mustard
1/4 teaspoon celery seeds

In small bowl combine mayonnaise, sugar, vinegar, milk, salt, dry mustard and celery seeds. Cover; chill.   *Makes about 1¹/4 cups*

Caesar Dressing

1 cup HELLMANN'S® or BEST
   FOODS® Real, Light or
   Cholesterol Free Reduced
   Calorie Mayonnaise
3 tablespoons milk

2 tablespoons cider vinegar
2 tablespoons grated
   Parmesan cheese
1/2 teaspoon sugar
1/8 teaspoon garlic powder

In small bowl combine mayonnaise, milk, vinegar, Parmesan, sugar and garlic powder. Cover; chill.   *Makes about 1¹/4 cups*

Nutmeg Dressing

1 cup HELLMANN'S® or BEST
   FOODS® Real, Light or
   Cholesterol Free Reduced
   Calorie Mayonnaise

2 tablespoons sugar
1/2 teaspoon nutmeg
1 cup (8 ounces) vanilla
   yogurt

In small bowl combine mayonnaise, sugar and nutmeg until smooth. Fold in yogurt. Cover; chill. Serve with fresh fruit.

Makes 2 cups

SANDWICHES

Welsh Rarebit

1/2 cup HELLMANN'S® or BEST
  FOODS® Real, Light or
  Cholesterol Free Reduced
  Calorie Mayonnaise
3 tablespoons flour
1/2 teaspoon dry mustard
1/2 teaspoon Worcestershire
  sauce

3/4 cup beer
2 cups (8 ounces) shredded
  Cheddar cheese
8 slices white or whole wheat
  bread, toasted, halved
  diagonally
3 large tomatoes, cut into
  16 slices

In 2-quart saucepan combine mayonnaise, flour, dry mustard and
Worcestershire sauce. Stirring constantly, cook over low heat
1 minute. Gradually stir in beer until thick and smooth (do not
boil). Stir in cheese until melted. Arrange 4 toast halves and 4
tomato slices alternately on each of 4 serving plates; spoon on
cheese sauce. Serve immediately.   *Makes 4 servings*

Microwave Directions: In 2-quart microwavable bowl combine
mayonnaise, flour, dry mustard and Worcestershire sauce.
Gradually stir in beer and cheese. Microwave on HIGH (100%),
4 minutes, stirring vigorously after each minute. Serve as above.

Welsh Rarebit

Shrimp Louis Muffins

1 cup HELLMANN'S® or BEST FOODS® Real, Light or Cholesterol Free Reduced Calorie Mayonnaise
1/2 cup chili sauce
1 teaspoon lemon juice
1 teaspoon prepared horseradish
1/2 teaspoon grated onion
1/8 teaspoon salt
1/8 teaspoon freshly ground pepper
4 Thomas' original flavor English muffins, split, toasted and buttered
Lettuce leaves
4 hard-cooked eggs, sliced
3/4 pound medium shrimp, shelled, deveined and cooked

In small bowl combine mayonnaise, chili sauce, lemon juice, horseradish, onion, salt and pepper until blended. Cover; chill. Top each muffin half with lettuce, egg slices, shrimp and dressing. *Makes 4 servings*

Cranberry Turkey Sandwiches

1/2 cup HELLMANN'S® or BEST FOODS® Real, Light or Cholesterol Free Reduced Calorie Mayonnaise
1/2 cup grated Parmesan cheese
4 slices firm white bread, toasted
8 slices cooked turkey
1/2 cup prepared cranberry sauce

In small bowl combine mayonnaise and Parmesan. Top each bread slice with 2 slices turkey and 2 tablespoons cranberry sauce. Spread mayonnaise mixture over each. Broil 6 inches from heat 2 to 3 minutes or until lightly browned.
Makes 4 sandwiches

Shrimp Louis Muffins

Microwave Mexicali Franks

6 frankfurters, sliced
 crosswise
½ cup chopped onion
1 can (6 ounces) tomato paste
1 can (4 ounces) chopped
 green chilies, undrained
½ cup HELLMANN'S® or BEST
 FOODS® Real, Light or
 Cholesterol Free Reduced
 Calorie Mayonnaise

6 frankfurter rolls, split and
 toasted
½ cup (2 ounces) shredded
 Cheddar cheese

Microwave Directions: In 2-quart microwavable dish combine frankfurters, onion, tomato paste and chilies. Microwave on HIGH (100%) 4 minutes, stirring after 1 minute. Stir in mayonnaise. Spoon into rolls; sprinkle with cheese. Arrange in circle on microwavable platter. Microwave 2 minutes or until hot.

Makes 6 servings

Pepperoni Pizzas

1 cup (4 ounces) shredded
 mozzarella cheese
1 cup sliced pitted ripe olives
4 ounces pepperoni, chopped
½ cup HELLMANN'S® or BEST
 FOODS® Real, Light or
 Cholesterol Free Reduced
 Calorie Mayonnaise

¼ teaspoon dried Italian
 seasoning
4 Thomas' English muffins,
 split and toasted

In medium bowl combine cheese, olives, pepperoni, mayonnaise and Italian seasoning. Spoon onto muffin halves. Broil 6 inches from heat 5 minutes or until browned. *Makes 8 pizzas*

Microwave Directions: Prepare pizzas as above. Arrange in circle on microwavable platter. Microwave on HIGH (100%) 2 minutes or until cheese melts.

Monte Cristo Sandwiches

1/3 cup HELLMANN'S® or BEST
   FOODS® Real, Light or
   Cholesterol Free Reduced
   Calorie Mayonnaise
1/4 teaspoon nutmeg
1/8 teaspoon freshly ground
   pepper
12 slices white bread, crusts
   removed

6 slices Swiss cheese
6 slices cooked ham
6 slices cooked chicken or
   turkey
2 eggs
1/2 cup milk

In small bowl combine mayonnaise, nutmeg and pepper; spread
on 1 side of each bread slice. Arrange cheese, ham and chicken
on mayonnaise sides of 6 bread slices; top with remaining bread,
mayonnaise-sides down. Cut sandwiches diagonally into quarters.
In small bowl beat together eggs and milk; dip sandwich quarters
into egg mixture. Cook on preheated greased griddle or in skillet,
turning once, 4 to 5 minutes or until browned and heated
through.   *Makes 24 sandwiches*

Newfangled Grilled Cheese Sandwich

1 tablespoon HELLMANN'S®
   or BEST FOODS® Real,
   Light or Cholesterol Free
   Reduced Calorie
   Mayonnaise

Pinch of dried oregano,
   basil, tarragon or dillweed
2 slices bread
1 slice (1 ounce) cheese
1 tomato slice (optional)

In small cup blend mayonnaise with a pinch of dried herb;
spread on 1 side of each bread slice. Assemble sandwich using
cheese and tomato, with mayonnaise on outside. Cook on
preheated griddle or in skillet, turning once, until cheese is
melted and bread is lightly toasted.   *Makes 1 sandwich*

Open-Faced Zucchini and Roasted Red Pepper Melt

1/2 cup HELLMANN'S® or BEST FOODS® Real, Light or Cholesterol Free Reduced Calorie Mayonnaise
1 clove garlic, minced or pressed
1 tablespoon chopped fresh basil *or* 1 teaspoon dried basil
1 1/2 teaspoons chopped fresh oregano *or* 1/2 teaspoon dried oregano
1/2 teaspoon freshly ground pepper

1 loaf (14 inches) Italian bread, sliced lengthwise and cut crosswise in half
1 zucchini,* sliced diagonally into 8 slices
1 jar (7 1/4 ounces) roasted red peppers, drained and cut into quarters *or* 2 medium red peppers, roasted, peeled and cut into quarters
1/2 cup (2 ounces) shredded mozzarella cheese

In small bowl blend mayonnaise, garlic, basil, oregano and pepper. Brush cut sides of bread with half of the mayonnaise mixture. Broil 5 inches from heat 2 minutes or until golden brown. Remove and set aside. Brush zucchini slices with remaining mayonnaise mixture. Broil 2 minutes, turning once. Top each slice of bread alternately with zucchini and red pepper. Sprinkle with cheese. Broil 1 to 2 minutes or until golden brown and cheese melts.   *Makes 4 sandwiches*

*One medium eggplant, peeled and sliced crosswise, may be substituted for zucchini.

Open-Faced Zucchini and Roasted Red Pepper Melt

Tuna Burgers

1 can (6½ ounces) tuna,
  drained and flaked
¾ cup dry bread crumbs
1 egg, slightly beaten
½ cup minced celery
⅓ cup HELLMANN'S® or BEST
  FOODS® Real, Light or
  Cholesterol Free Reduced
  Calorie Mayonnaise

¼ cup minced onion
1 teaspoon lemon juice
  Lettuce leaves
  Sliced tomato
4 Thomas' honey wheat
  English muffins, split,
  toasted and buttered
  Tartar sauce (optional)

In medium bowl combine tuna, bread crumbs, egg, celery, mayonnaise, onion and lemon juice until blended. Cover; chill 1 hour. Shape into 4 patties. Heat lightly greased skillet over medium heat. Add tuna patties; cook, turning once, about 6 minutes or until lightly browned. Place lettuce, tuna burger and tomato on each bottom muffin half. Top with remaining muffin halves. If desired, serve with tartar sauce.

Makes 4 sandwiches

Reuben Sandwiches

8 slices rye bread
¾ cup Russian Dressing (recipe
  on page 46)
4 slices Swiss cheese
8 ounces sliced, cooked
  corned beef

1 cup sauerkraut, well drained
¼ cup HELLMANN'S® or BEST
  FOODS® Real, Light or
  Cholesterol Free Reduced
  Calorie Mayonnaise

Spread 4 bread slices with some of the dressing. Top with cheese and corned beef. Toss sauerkraut with remaining dressing; spoon over corned beef. Cover with remaining bread. Spread outside of sandwiches with mayonnaise. Cook on preheated griddle or in skillet, turning once, 4 to 5 minutes or until browned and heated through.

Makes 4 sandwiches

Rachel Sandwiches

3/4 cup HELLMANN'S® or BEST
　FOODS® Real, Light or
　Cholesterol Free Reduced
　Calorie Mayonnaise,
　divided
1 tablespoon cider vinegar
1 1/2 teaspoons sugar
3/4 teaspoon dry mustard

1/2 teaspoon celery salt
3 cups finely shredded
　cabbage
4 slices Swiss cheese
8 ounces sliced cooked
　pastrami
8 slices whole wheat bread

In medium bowl combine 1/2 cup of the mayonnaise, the vinegar, sugar, dry mustard and celery salt. Add cabbage; toss to coat well. Arrange cheese and meat on 4 bread slices; top with cabbage mixture. Cover with remaining bread. Spread outside of sandwiches with remaining 1/4 cup mayonnaise. Cook on preheated griddle or in skillet, turning once, until browned and heated through. *Makes 4 sandwiches*

Fish Stick Sandwiches

1/2 cup HELLMANN'S® or BEST
　FOODS® Real, Light or
　Cholesterol Free Reduced
　Calorie Mayonnaise
1/2 cup (2 ounces) shredded
　process American cheese
2 tablespoons sweet pickle
　relish

2 tablespoons chopped onion
1 package (9 ounces) frozen
　fish sticks, cooked
　(12 sticks)
4 tomato slices
4 hamburger rolls, split and
　toasted

In small bowl combine mayonnaise, cheese, relish and onion; set aside. Arrange 3 fish sticks and 1 tomato slice on bottom of each roll; spoon on mayonnaise mixture. Place on baking sheet. Bake in 400°F oven 10 minutes or until cheese melts. Cover with tops of rolls. *Makes 4 sandwiches*

ENTRÉES

Magically Moist Chicken

1 chicken (2½ to 3½
   pounds), cut into pieces
½ cup HELLMANN'S® or BEST
   FOODS® Real, Light or
   Cholesterol Free Reduced
   Calorie Mayonnaise

1¼ cups Italian seasoned bread
   crumbs

Brush chicken on all sides with mayonnaise. Place bread crumbs
in large plastic food bag. Add chicken 1 piece at a time; shake to
coat well. Arrange on rack in broiler pan. Bake in 425°F oven
about 40 minutes or until golden brown and tender.

Makes 4 servings

Marvelous Marinated London Broil

½ cup HELLMANN'S® or BEST
   FOODS® Real, Light or
   Cholesterol Free Reduced
   Calorie Mayonnaise
⅓ cup soy sauce
¼ cup lemon juice
2 tablespoons prepared
   mustard

1 clove garlic, minced or
   pressed
½ teaspoon ground ginger
¼ teaspoon freshly ground
   pepper
1 beef top round steak
   (3 pounds), 2 inches
   thick

In large shallow dish combine mayonnaise, soy sauce, lemon
juice, mustard, garlic, ginger and pepper. Add steak, turning to
coat. Cover; marinate in refrigerator several hours or overnight.
Grill or broil about 6 inches from heat, turning once, 25 to 30
minutes or until desired doneness. To serve, slice diagonally
across grain.

Makes 6 to 8 servings

Salmon with Cilantro-Lime Sauce

³/₄ cup HELLMANN'S® or BEST FOODS® Real, Light or Cholesterol Free Reduced Calorie Mayonnaise
¹/₂ cup chopped fresh cilantro *or* ¹/₄ cup chopped fresh dill
2 tablespoons lime juice

1 medium tomato, seeded and diced
4 salmon or halibut steaks (about 6 ounces each), ³/₄ inch thick
Mazola No Stick cooking spray

In medium bowl combine mayonnaise, cilantro and lime juice. Transfer ¹/₂ cup to a small bowl and stir in tomato; set aside. Brush fish steaks with remaining mayonnaise mixture. Spray large skillet with cooking spray. Heat over medium-high heat. Add fish. Cook, turning once, 8 minutes or until fish is firm but moist. Serve with cilantro-lime sauce. *Makes 4 servings*

Grill Method: Grill fish steaks 6 inches from heat, turning once, about 8 minutes or until firm but moist.

Turkey Divine

¹/₂ cup HELLMANN'S® or BEST FOODS® Real, Light or Cholesterol Free Reduced Calorie Mayonnaise
¹/₂ teaspoon prepared mustard
1¹/₂ cups cubed cooked turkey
1 package (9 ounces) frozen cut broccoli, thawed and drained

¹/₂ cup (2 ounces) shredded Jarlsberg or Swiss cheese
¹/₄ cup chopped onion
1 egg white, stiffly beaten

In small bowl combine mayonnaise and mustard. In medium bowl combine turkey, broccoli, cheese, onion and ¹/₄ cup of the mayonnaise mixture. Spoon into 1-quart casserole. Fold remaining mayonnaise mixture into beaten egg white. Spread evenly over top of casserole. Bake in 400°F oven 25 minutes or until golden. *Makes 4 servings*

Salmon with Cilantro-Lime Sauce

Grilled Salmon with Cucumber Sauce

3/4 cup HELLMANN'S® or BEST
   FOODS® Real, Light or
   Cholesterol Free Reduced
   Calorie Mayonnaise
1/4 cup snipped fresh dill *or*
1 tablespoon dried
   dillweed

1 tablespoon lemon juice
6 salmon steaks (4 ounces
   each), 3/4 inch thick
1 small cucumber, seeded and
   chopped
1/2 cup chopped radishes
   Lemon wedges

In medium bowl combine mayonnaise, dill and lemon juice; reserve 1/2 cup for sauce. Brush fish steaks with remaining mayonnaise mixture. Grill 6 inches from heat, turning and brushing frequently with mayonnaise mixture, 6 to 8 minutes or until fish is firm but moist. Stir cucumber and radishes into reserved mayonnaise mixture. Serve fish with cucumber sauce and lemon wedges. *Makes 6 servings*

Turkey Casserole Olé

1 can (14 1/2 or 16 ounces)
   whole tomatoes,
   undrained
1 package (1.9 ounces) Knorr
   cream of mushroom soup
   and recipe mix
1/2 cup sour cream
1/2 cup HELLMANN'S® or BEST
   FOODS® Real, Light or
   Cholesterol Free Reduced
   Calorie Mayonnaise
1/2 cup chicken broth

4 to 5 pickled jalapeño
   peppers, seeded and finely
   chopped
1 medium onion, finely
   chopped
3 cups shredded cooked
   turkey
2 cups (8 ounces) shredded
   Cheddar cheese, divided
3 cups coarsely crushed corn
   chips, divided

In medium bowl crush whole tomatoes with fork. Stir in soup mix, sour cream, mayonnaise, chicken broth, jalapeño peppers, onion, turkey and 1 cup of the cheese. Add 2 cups of the corn chips. Spoon into 11×7×1 1/2-inch baking dish. Sprinkle with remaining 1 cup cheese and 1 cup chips. Bake in 350°F oven 20 minutes or until heated through. *Makes 6 servings*

Simply Wonderful Stir-Fry Dinner

¹/₃ cup HELLMANN'S® or BEST FOODS® Real, Light or Cholesterol Free Reduced Calorie Mayonnaise
2 tablespoons soy sauce
1 teaspoon grated fresh ginger
1 clove garlic, minced or pressed
¹/₈ teaspoon crushed dried red pepper

12 ounces lean boneless pork *or* boneless skinless chicken breasts, cut into thin strips
4 ounces snow peas, trimmed
1 medium red bell pepper, cut into thin strips
2 green onions, thinly sliced

In large bowl combine mayonnaise, soy sauce, ginger, garlic and dried red pepper. Add pork, snow peas, red bell pepper and green onions; toss to coat well. Heat large skillet over medium-high heat. Add pork mixture; stir-fry 4 to 5 minutes or until pork is tender.   *Makes 4 servings*

Coquilles St. Jacques

1¹/₂ cups (6 ounces) shredded Swiss cheese
²/₃ cup HELLMANN'S® or BEST FOODS® Real, Light or Cholesterol Free Reduced Calorie Mayonnaise
1 tablespoon chopped parsley
Mazola No Stick cooking spray

1 pound small scallops (bay)
¹/₂ pound fresh mushrooms, sliced
¹/₂ cup chopped onion
2 tablespoons dry sherry
2 tablespoons grated Parmesan cheese

In small bowl combine Swiss cheese, mayonnaise and parsley. Spray large skillet with cooking spray. Heat over medium-high heat. Add scallops. Stirring frequently, cook 2 minutes. Remove and drain well. In same skillet combine mushrooms, onion and dry sherry. Stirring frequently, cook 3 to 4 minutes or until tender. Remove from heat. Stir in scallops and cheese mixture until well blended. Spoon into 4 individual baking or shell-shaped dishes. Sprinkle each with Parmesan. Broil 6 inches from heat 3 minutes or until lightly browned and heated through.
Makes 4 servings

Buffalo Turkey Kabobs

²/₃ cup HELLMANN'S® or BEST
FOODS® Real, Light or
Cholesterol Free Reduced
Calorie Mayonnaise,
divided
1 teaspoon hot pepper sauce
1 ¹/₂ pounds boneless turkey
breast, cut into 1-inch
cubes
2 red bell peppers *or* 1 red
and 1 yellow bell pepper,
cut into 1-inch squares

2 medium onions, cut into
wedges
¹/₄ cup (1 ounce) crumbled
blue cheese
2 tablespoons milk
1 medium stalk celery, minced
1 medium carrot, minced

In medium bowl combine ¹/₃ cup of the mayonnaise and the hot
pepper sauce. Stir in turkey. Let stand at room temperature 20
minutes. On 6 skewers, alternately thread turkey, peppers and
onions. Grill or broil 5 inches from heat, brushing with
remaining mayonnaise mixture and turning frequently, 12 to 15
minutes. Meanwhile, in small bowl blend remaining ¹/₃ cup
mayonnaise with the blue cheese and milk. Stir in celery and
carrot. Serve with kabobs. *Makes 6 servings*

Note: For best results, use Real Mayonnaise. If using Light or
Cholesterol Free Reduced Calorie Mayonnaise, use sauce the
same day.

Microwave Flounder au Gratin

¹/₄ cup dry bread crumbs
¹/₄ cup grated Parmesan cheese
1 pound flounder or sole
fillets

¹/₄ cup HELLMANN'S® or BEST
FOODS® Real, Light or
Cholesterol Free Reduced
Calorie Mayonnaise

Microwave Directions: In shallow dish or on sheet of waxed paper
combine crumbs and Parmesan. Brush both sides of fillets with
mayonnaise; coat with crumb mixture. Arrange in single layer in
11×7×1¹/₂-inch microwavable dish. Cover with waxed paper.
Microwave on HIGH (100%) 6 minutes or until fish is firm but
moist. *Makes 4 servings*

Buffalo Turkey Kabobs

Mexican Hamburger Topping

$^1/_2$ cup HELLMANN's® or BEST
FOODS® Real, Light or
Cholesterol Free Reduced
Calorie Mayonnaise
$^1/_2$ cup prepared chunky salsa,
drained

$^1/_2$ cup (2 ounces) shredded
Cheddar cheese
$^1/_2$ cup refried beans

In small bowl combine mayonnaise, salsa, cheese and beans.
Serve with hamburgers.   *Makes about 1²/₃ cups*

VARIATIONS

Bacon Hamburger Topping: Combine 1 cup mayonnaise and $^1/_4$
cup crumbled cooked bacon or real bacon bits. Makes about 1
cup.

Green Onion Hamburger Topping: Combine 1 cup mayonnaise
and $^1/_4$ cup sliced green onions. Makes about 1 cup.

Chicken with Zesty Tuna Sauce

1 can (6$^1/_2$ ounces) tuna,
drained
$^1/_2$ cup HELLMANN'S® or BEST
FOODS® Real, Light or
Cholesterol Free Reduced
Calorie Mayonnaise
$^1/_3$ cup milk
1 tablespoon capers, rinsed
and drained

2 anchovy fillets
2 tablespoons lemon juice
1 pound boneless skinless
chicken breasts, cooked
and sliced
3 tomatoes, sliced
1 tablespoon chopped parsley

In food processor or blender container place tuna, mayonnaise,
milk, capers and anchovy fillets. Process until smooth. Add
lemon juice; process until blended. On large serving platter
alternately arrange chicken and tomato slices, overlapping slightly
to form a circle. Top with tuna sauce. Sprinkle with parsley.

Makes 4 servings

*Top to bottom: Bacon, Mexican and
Green Onion Hamburger Toppings*

Spareribs with Tex-Mex Barbecue Sauce

6 pounds pork spareribs, cut
   into 2-rib portions
1/2 cup HELLMANN'S® or BEST
   FOODS® Real, Light or
   Cholesterol Free Reduced
   Calorie Mayonnaise

1/2 cup ketchup
1/4 cup Worcestershire sauce
3 tablespoons chili powder
1 clove garlic, minced or
   pressed
1/8 teaspoon hot pepper sauce

In large shallow roasting pan arrange ribs in single layer on a rack. Roast in 325°F oven 1½ hours or until tender. Meanwhile, prepare Tex-Mex barbecue sauce: In small bowl with wire whisk combine mayonnaise, ketchup, Worcestershire sauce, chili powder, garlic and hot pepper sauce until smooth. Brush on ribs, turning frequently, during last 20 minutes of roasting time.

Makes 6 servings

Homestyle Barbecue Sauce: Follow recipe for Tex-Mex barbecue sauce. Omit chili powder and garlic. Add 1/4 cup prepared mustard and 1/4 cup Karo dark corn syrup or 1/4 cup firmly packed brown sugar. Makes 1½ cups.

Sweet and Sour Barbecue Sauce: Follow recipe for Tex-Mex barbecue sauce. Omit Worcestershire sauce, chili powder, garlic and hot pepper sauce. Add 3/4 cup apricot preserves, 1/4 cup soy sauce and 1 teaspoon ground ginger. Makes 1½ cups.

Quick and Crispy Cutlets

2 cups seasoned dry stuffing
   mix, coarsely crushed
1/4 cup HELLMANN'S® or BEST
   FOODS® Real, Light or
   Cholesterol Free Reduced
   Calorie Mayonnaise

1 tablespoon minced onion
1 pound chicken, pork or
   turkey cutlets, about
   1/4 inch thick

Place stuffing mix in shallow dish or on waxed paper. In small bowl combine mayonnaise and onion. Brush both sides of cutlets with mayonnaise mixture; coat with stuffing mix. Arrange in single layer in shallow baking pan or on rack in broiler pan. Bake in 425°F oven 10 to 15 minutes or until cutlets are golden and tender.

Makes 4 servings

Almond-Baked Fish Fillets

1/2 cup finely chopped
   unblanched almonds
1/4 cup dry bread crumbs
1/4 teaspoon salt
1/8 teaspoon freshly ground
   pepper
1 pound fish fillets, such as
   flounder or sole

1/4 cup HELLMANN'S® or BEST
   FOODS® Real, Light or
   Cholesterol Free Reduced
   Calorie Mayonnaise
Lemon wedges (optional)

In shallow dish combine almonds, crumbs, salt and pepper. Brush both sides of fillets with mayonnaise; coat with crumb mixture. Arrange in single layer in shallow baking pan or on rack in broiler pan. Bake in 425°F oven until fish is golden and firm but moist. (Allow 5 to 6 minutes for each 1/2-inch thickness.) If desired, serve with lemon wedges. *Makes 4 servings*

Turkey 'n Stuff

2 cups cubed cooked turkey
1 cup chopped celery
1 small onion, chopped
1 cup dry stuffing mix*
1/2 cup slivered almonds,
   toasted, divided
1/2 cup HELLMANN'S® or BEST
   FOODS® Real, Light or
   Cholesterol Free Reduced
   Calorie Mayonnaise

1/2 cup sour cream
1 to 2 tablespoons lemon
   juice
1 teaspoon Worcestershire
   sauce

In large bowl combine turkey, celery, onion, stuffing mix, 1/4 cup of the almonds, the mayonnaise, sour cream, lemon juice and Worcestershire sauce. Spoon into 1 1/2-quart casserole; sprinkle with remaining 1/4 cup almonds. Bake in 350°F oven 20 minutes or until heated through. *Makes 4 to 6 servings*

*One cup leftover prepared stuffing may be substituted for dry stuffing mix.

VEGETABLES

Hollandaise Sauce

³/₄ cup HELLMANN'S® or BEST
   FOODS® Real, Light or
   Cholesterol Free Reduced
   Calorie Mayonnaise
¹/₃ cup milk

¹/₄ teaspoon salt
   Dash freshly ground pepper
1 teaspoon grated lemon peel
1 tablespoon lemon juice

In small saucepan combine mayonnaise, milk, salt and pepper
until smooth. Stirring constantly, cook over low heat about 3
minutes or just until heated. Stir in lemon peel and lemon juice.
Serve with cooked asparagus, broccoli or other vegetables.

Makes about 1 cup

Potato Pancakes

2 cups coarsely shredded
   peeled potatoes
¹/₂ cup HELLMANN'S® or BEST
   FOODS® Real, Light or
   Cholesterol Free Reduced
   Calorie Mayonnaise

2 tablespoons grated onion
1 tablespoon Mazola corn oil
   Applesauce (optional)

Dry potatoes well between paper towels. In medium bowl
combine potatoes, mayonnaise and onion. In large skillet heat
corn oil over medium-high heat. Add potato mixture by
tablespoonfuls, a few at a time, to skillet; flatten slightly. Fry,
turning once, 4 minutes or until golden brown. Drain on paper
towels. If desired, serve with applesauce.

Makes about 15 (3-inch) pancakes

Hollandaise Sauce

Zucchini and Carrot au Gratin

1/4 cup HELLMANN'S® or BEST FOODS® Real, Light or Cholesterol Free Reduced Calorie Mayonnaise
1/4 cup minced onion
2 tablespoons flour
1 tablespoon chopped parsley
3/4 teaspoon salt
1/4 teaspoon dried Italian seasoning

Dash freshly ground pepper
1 cup milk
3 medium carrots, sliced, cooked and drained
2 medium zucchini, sliced, cooked and drained
1/2 cup fresh bread crumbs
1/4 cup grated Parmesan cheese
1 tablespoon Mazola margarine, melted

In 1-quart saucepan combine mayonnaise, onion, flour, parsley, salt, Italian seasoning and pepper. Stirring constantly, cook over medium heat 1 minute. Gradually stir in milk until smooth. Stirring constantly, cook until thick (do not boil). In medium bowl combine carrots and zucchini. Add sauce; toss to coat well. Spoon into shallow 1-quart broilerproof casserole. In small bowl combine bread crumbs, Parmesan and margarine; sprinkle over vegetables. Broil 6 inches from heat 3 minutes or until golden.

Makes 4 to 6 servings

Crispy Eggplant

1/2 cup HELLMANN'S® or BEST FOODS® Real, Light or Cholesterol Free Reduced Calorie Mayonnaise
1 tablespoon instant minced onion
1/4 teaspoon salt

1/3 cup dry bread crumbs
1/3 cup grated Parmesan cheese
1/2 teaspoon dried Italian seasoning
1 medium eggplant (about 1 pound), cut crosswise into 1/2-inch slices

In small bowl combine mayonnaise, onion and salt. In shallow dish or on sheet of waxed paper combine crumbs, Parmesan and Italian seasoning. Brush both sides of eggplant slices with mayonnaise mixture; coat with crumb mixture. Arrange in single layer on baking sheet. Bake in 425°F oven 15 minutes or until browned.

Makes 4 to 6 servings

Note: For make-ahead convenience, prepare eggplant as above. Cover; refrigerate. Bake just before serving.

Potato Topping Olé

2/3 cup HELLMANN'S® or BEST
   FOODS® Real, Light or
   Cholesterol Free Reduced
   Calorie Mayonnaise
1/2 cup prepared salsa, drained
1/2 cup refried beans

1/2 cup (2 ounces) shredded
   Monterey Jack cheese
   with jalapeño peppers
3 tablespoons chopped fresh
   cilantro

In small bowl combine mayonnaise, salsa, beans, cheese and
cilantro. Serve over baked potatoes.   *Makes about 1 1/2 cups*

Microwave Curried Cauliflower

1 can (10 3/4 ounces) condensed
   cream of mushroom soup
1 cup (4 ounces) shredded
   Cheddar cheese
1/3 cup HELLMANN'S® or BEST
   FOODS® Real, Light or
   Cholesterol Free Reduced
   Calorie Mayonnaise

1 teaspoon curry powder
1 large head cauliflower,
   broken into florets,
   cooked and drained
1/4 cup dry bread crumbs
2 tablespoons Mazola
   margarine, melted

In 1-quart microwavable bowl combine soup, cheese, mayonnaise
and curry. Microwave on HIGH (100%) 3 minutes or until hot,
stirring after each minute. Pour over hot cauliflower. In small
bowl mix bread crumbs and margarine; sprinkle over cauliflower.
Makes 6 to 8 servings

Sun Valley Potato Fries

2 large baking potatoes
1/4 cup HELLMANN'S® or BEST
   FOODS® Real, Light or
   Cholesterol Free Reduced
   Calorie Mayonnaise

Salt to taste

Cut potatoes into 1/4-inch sticks. Spoon mayonnaise into large
plastic food bag. Add potatoes; shake to coat well. Arrange in
single layer in jelly-roll pan so potatoes do not touch. Sprinkle
with salt to taste. Bake in 400°F oven, turning once with spatula,
20 minutes or until golden brown and crisp.   *Makes 6 servings*

Pizza Potato Topping

²/₃ cup HELLMANN'S® or BEST
   FOODS® Real, Light or
   Cholesterol Free Reduced
   Calorie Mayonnaise
½ cup finely chopped
   pepperoni

¼ cup (1 ounce) shredded
   mozzarella cheese
¼ cup grated Parmesan cheese
3 tablespoons prepared pizza
   sauce

In small bowl combine mayonnaise, pepperoni, cheeses and
pizza sauce. Serve over baked potatoes.

Makes about 1¹/₃ cups

Broccoli-Cheese Potato Topping

1 cup HELLMANN'S® or BEST
   FOODS® Real, Light or
   Cholesterol Free Reduced
   Calorie Mayonnaise

1 package (10 ounces) frozen
   chopped broccoli, thawed
   and drained
1 cup (4 ounces) shredded
   Cheddar cheese

In small bowl combine mayonnaise, broccoli and cheese. Serve
over baked potatoes.

Makes about 2¹/₄ cups

Bacon-Cheddar Potato Topping

1 cup HELLMANN's® or BEST
   FOODS® Real, Light or
   Cholesterol Free Reduced
   Calorie Mayonnaise

½ cup (2 ounces) shredded
   Cheddar cheese
¼ cup crumbled cooked bacon
   or real bacon bits

In small bowl combine mayonnaise, cheese and bacon. Serve
over baked potatoes.

Makes about 1¹/₄ cups

VARIATIONS

Parmesan Cheese Potato Topping: Combine 1 cup mayonnaise and
½ cup grated Parmesan cheese. Makes about 1¹/₄ cups.

Green Onion Potato Topping: Combine 1 cup mayonnaise and ¼
cup sliced green onions. Makes about 1 cup.

*Top to bottom: Pizza, Broccoli-Cheese and
Bacon-Cheddar Potato Toppings*

Vegetables Italiano

1 cup Italian seasoned bread
  crumbs
1/3 cup grated Parmesan cheese
2/3 cup HELLMANN'S® or BEST
  FOODS® Real, Light or
  Cholesterol Free Reduced
  Calorie Mayonnaise

6 cups assorted vegetables:
  broccoli florets, carrot
  slices, cauliflower florets,
  small mushrooms, green
  and/or red bell pepper
  strips, yellow squash slices
  and/or zucchini strips

In plastic food bag combine crumbs and Parmesan; shake to blend well. In another bag combine mayonnaise and vegetables; shake to coat well. Add mayonnaise-coated vegetables, half at a time, to crumb mixture; shake to coat well. Arrange in single layer on ungreased cookie sheet so that pieces do not touch. Bake in 425°F oven 10 minutes or until golden.

Makes about 8 servings

Saucy Skillet Potatoes

1 tablespoon Mazola
  margarine
1 cup chopped onions
1/2 cup HELLMANN's® or BEST
  FOODS® Real, Light or
  Cholesterol Free Reduced
  Calorie Mayonnaise
1/3 cup cider vinegar
1 tablespoon sugar

1 teaspoon salt
1/4 teaspoon freshly ground
  pepper
4 medium potatoes, cooked,
  peeled and sliced
1 tablespoon chopped parsley
1 tablespoon crumbled
  cooked bacon or real
  bacon bits

In large skillet melt margarine over medium heat. Add onions; cook 2 to 3 minutes or until tender-crisp. Stir in mayonnaise, vinegar, sugar, salt and pepper. Add potatoes; cook, stirring constantly, 2 minutes or until hot (do not boil). Sprinkle with parsley and bacon.

Makes 6 to 8 servings

Vegetables Italiano

Easy Spinach Soufflé

¹/₂ cup HELLMANN'S® or BEST
FOODS® Real, Light or
Cholesterol Free Reduced
Calorie Mayonnaise
¹/₄ cup flour
2 tablespoons grated onion
³/₄ teaspoon salt
¹/₄ teaspoon nutmeg
¹/₄ teaspoon freshly ground
pepper

1 cup milk
1 package (10 ounces) frozen
chopped spinach, thawed
and well drained on paper
towels
4 eggs, separated
¹/₄ teaspoon cream of tartar

Preheat oven to 400°F. Grease 2-quart soufflé dish. In 3-quart saucepan combine mayonnaise, flour, onion, salt, nutmeg and pepper. Stirring constantly, cook over medium heat 1 minute. Gradually stir in milk until smooth. Stirring constantly, cook until thick. Remove from heat. Stir in spinach. Beat in egg yolks. In small bowl with mixer at high speed, beat egg whites with cream of tartar until stiff peaks form. Gently fold into spinach mixture. Spoon into prepared dish. Place on lowest rack of oven. Immediately reduce oven temperature to 375°F. Bake 40 minutes or until top is puffed and golden brown. Serve immediately.

Makes 4 to 6 servings

Blue Ribbon Vegetables

¹/₂ cup HELLMANN's® or BEST
FOODS® Real, Light or
Cholesterol Free Reduced
Calorie Mayonnaise
2 to 4 tablespoons milk
1 tablespoon Dijon-style
mustard

Dash freshly ground pepper
2 packages (10 ounces each)
frozen vegetables
(broccoli spears, green
beans or cauliflower)
2 tablespoons grated
Parmesan cheese

In small bowl combine mayonnaise, milk, mustard and pepper; set aside. Cook vegetables according to package directions; drain. Spoon sauce over hot vegetables. Sprinkle with Parmesan.

Makes 6 to 8 servings

Tomatoes Genoa

1/3 cup dry bread crumbs
3 tablespoons grated
  Parmesan cheese
1/4 cup HELLMANN'S® or BEST
  FOODS® Real, Light or
  Cholesterol Free Reduced
  Calorie Mayonnaise

1 tablespoon finely chopped
  fresh basil *or* 1 teaspoon
  dried basil
1 pound tomatoes, cut into
  1/2-inch slices

In shallow dish combine crumbs and Parmesan until well mixed.
In small bowl combine mayonnaise and basil. Brush both sides
of tomato slices with mayonnaise mixture; coat with crumb
mixture. Arrange in single layer on rack in broiler pan so that
pieces do not touch. Bake in 425°F oven 10 to 15 minutes or until
lightly browned.   *Makes 4 servings*

Microwave Potato Pie

3 cups prepared fresh or
  instant mashed potatoes
1/2 cup (2 ounces) shredded
  Swiss cheese
1/2 cup HELLMANN'S® or BEST
  FOODS® Real, Light or
  Cholesterol Free Reduced
  Calorie Mayonnaise

1/4 cup chopped green onions
1 egg, slightly beaten
Paprika

Microwave Directions: With mixer or wire whisk beat potatoes,
cheese, mayonnaise, green onions and egg. Spoon into 1-quart
microwavable dish. Sprinkle lightly with paprika. Microwave on
MEDIUM (50%) 20 minutes or until hot, rotating dish 1/4 turn
every 5 minutes. Let stand 5 minutes.   *Makes 4 to 6 servings*

BREADS & DESSERTS

Chocolate Mayonnaise Cake

2 cups flour
2/3 cup unsweetened cocoa
1 1/4 teaspoons baking soda
1/4 teaspoon baking powder
3 eggs
1 2/3 cups sugar

1 teaspoon vanilla
1 cup HELLMANN'S® or BEST
FOODS® Real, Light or
Cholesterol Free Reduced
Calorie Mayonnaise
1 1/3 cups water

Grease and flour bottoms of 2 (9×1½-inch) round cake pans. In medium bowl combine flour, cocoa, baking soda and baking powder; set aside. In large bowl with mixer at high speed, beat eggs, sugar and vanilla, scraping bowl occasionally, 3 minutes or until smooth and creamy. Reduce speed to low; beat in mayonnaise until blended. Add flour mixture in 4 additions alternately with water, beginning and ending with flour mixture. Pour into prepared pans. Bake in 350°F oven 30 to 35 minutes or until·cake springs back when touched lightly in center. Cool in pans on wire racks 10 minutes. Remove from pans; cool completely on racks. Fill and frost as desired.

Makes 1 (9-inch) layer cake

Microwave Directions: Follow recipe for Chocolate Mayonnaise Cake. Line bottoms of 2 (8×2½-inch) round microwavable cake pans with circles of waxed paper or microwavable paper towels. Pour batter into prepared cake pans. Microwave 1 layer at a time. Place 1 cake pan on inverted microwavable pie plate in microwave oven. Microwave on MEDIUM (50%) 5 minutes. If cake appears to be rising unevenly, rotate pan during cooking. Microwave on HIGH (100%) 3 to 5 minutes longer or just until cake begins to set up on the outer edge. Center may appear to be slightly soft, but cake will firm up as it cools. Repeat with remaining layer. Let stand in pans 10 minutes on flat heatproof surface. Remove from pans; cool completely on wire racks.

Makes 1 (8-inch) layer cake

Chocolate Mayonnaise Cake

Quick Banana-Bran Bread

Mazola No Stick cooking
  spray
1 package (7 ounces) bran
  muffin mix
1/3 cup chopped nuts
1/4 cup flour
1/4 teaspoon cinnamon
1 egg, lightly beaten

1 ripe banana, mashed (about
  1/3 cup)
1/3 cup HELLMANN'S® or BEST
  FOODS® Real, Light or
  Cholesterol Free Reduced
  Calorie Mayonnaise
1/3 cup water

Spray 8 1/2 × 4 1/2 × 2 1/2-inch loaf pan with cooking spray. In medium bowl combine muffin mix, nuts, flour and cinnamon. In small bowl combine egg, banana, mayonnaise and water. Add to flour mixture, stirring just until moistened. Pour into prepared pan. Bake in 350°F oven 35 to 40 minutes or until toothpick inserted into center comes out clean. Cool in pan on wire rack 10 minutes. Remove from pan; cool completely on rack.

Makes 1 loaf

Our Very Best Bran Muffins

Mazola No Stick cooking
  spray
1 1/4 cups flour
1 tablespoon baking powder
1/4 teaspoon salt
1 1/2 cups whole or flake bran
  cereal
1 1/4 cups milk

3 tablespoons firmly packed
  light brown sugar
1/3 cup HELLMANN'S® or BEST
  FOODS® Real, Light or
  Cholesterol Free Reduced
  Calorie Mayonnaise
1 egg, lightly beaten
1/2 cup raisins

Spray 12 (2 1/2-inch) muffin pan cups with cooking spray. In small bowl combine flour, baking powder and salt. In large bowl combine bran cereal, milk and brown sugar. Let stand 1 to 2 minutes or until bran is softened. Stir in mayonnaise and egg until well blended. Add raisins. Stir in flour mixture just until moistened. Spoon into each prepared muffin pan cup. Bake in 400°F oven 25 minutes or until lightly browned. Immediately remove from pan. Serve warm.

Makes 12 muffins

*Top to bottom: Sunday Morn Cranberry-Orange
Bread (page 89); Our Very Best Bran Muffins,
California Date-Nut Muffins (page 89) and
Chili-Cheese Corn Muffins (page 92);
Quick Banana-Bran Bread*

Amazin' Raisin Cake

3 cups flour
2 cups sugar
2 teaspoons baking soda
1 1/2 teaspoons cinnamon
1/2 teaspoon nutmeg
1/2 teaspoon salt
1/4 teaspoon cloves
1 cup HELLMANN'S® or BEST FOODS® Real, Light or Cholesterol Free Reduced Calorie Mayonnaise

1/3 cup milk
2 eggs
3 cups coarsely chopped apples
1 cup raisins
1 cup coarsely chopped walnuts

Grease and flour 2 (9×1 1/2-inch) round cake pans. In large bowl combine flour, sugar, baking soda, cinnamon, nutmeg, salt and cloves. Add mayonnaise, milk and eggs. Beat at low speed 2 minutes, scraping bowl frequently. (Batter will be thick.) With spoon, stir in apples, raisins and nuts. Spoon into prepared pans. Bake in 350°F oven 40 to 45 minutes or until cake springs back when touched lightly in center. Cool in pans on wire racks 10 minutes. Remove from pans; cool completely on racks. Fill and frost as desired. *Makes 1 (9-inch) layer cake*

Microwave Brownie & Cake Mix

3 cups sugar
2 cups flour

2 cups unsweetened cocoa
1 1/2 teaspoons baking powder

Combine sugar, flour, cocoa and baking powder in large self-sealing plastic bag; seal. Shake until ingredients are thoroughly combined. (Or, thoroughly combine ingredients in large bowl.) Store mix in bag or in tightly covered container. Shake or mix well before using. *Makes 7 cups*

Microwave Brownies

Mazola No Stick cooking
spray
2 cups Microwave Brownie &
Cake Mix (recipe on
page 84)

2 eggs
1/2 cup HELLMANN'S® or BEST
FOODS® Real, Light or
Cholesterol Free Reduced
Calorie Mayonnaise

Microwave Directions: Spray 8×8×2-inch microwavable dish with cooking spray. In medium bowl combine mix, eggs and mayonnaise; stir until well blended. Spread evenly in prepared baking dish. Microwave on MEDIUM (50%), turning dish once, 6 minutes. Turn dish; microwave on HIGH (100%) 3 minutes longer or until surface is firm to the touch. Cool in dish on flat heatproof surface. Cut into 2-inch squares.

Makes 16 brownies

VARIATIONS

Microwave Rocky Road Brownies: Prepare Microwave Brownies batter, adding 1/2 cup chopped walnuts; spread evenly in prepared dish. Microwave on MEDIUM (50%), turning once, 6 minutes. Remove from oven. Sprinkle 1/2 cup semisweet chocolate chips over top, then 1 cup miniature marshmallows. Microwave on HIGH (100%) 4 minutes. With knife, swirl topping to marbleize. Cool.

Microwave Peanut Butter Streusel Brownies: Prepare Microwave Brownies batter; spread evenly in prepared dish. In medium bowl mix 1/2 cup uncooked quick cooking oats, 1/2 cup powdered sugar and 1/2 cup Skippy Super Chunk peanut butter until crumbly. Sprinkle over batter. Microwave on MEDIUM (50%), turning once, 6 minutes. Turn dish; microwave on HIGH (100%) 4 minutes longer. Cool.

Microwave German Chocolate Brownies: Prepare and cook Microwave Brownies as directed; cool. In medium microwavable bowl combine 20 caramels, 1 cup flaked coconut, 1/2 cup chopped pecans, 2 tablespoons Mazola margarine and 2 tablespoons milk. Microwave on HIGH (100%) 2 minutes; stir. Microwave 2 minutes longer; stir to melt caramels. Spread over cooled brownies.

Light 'n Luscious Cheesecake

1 tablespoon graham cracker
  crumbs
1 cup (8 ounces) lowfat
  cottage cheese
1 cup (8 ounces) plain lowfat
  yogurt
1/2 cup HELLMANN'S® or BEST
  FOODS® Real, Light or
  Cholesterol Free Reduced
  Calorie Mayonnaise

1/3 cup sugar
2 teaspoons grated lemon peel
1 tablespoon lemon juice
1 teaspoon vanilla
2 egg whites
  Raspberry Sauce (recipe
  follows)
  Fresh raspberries for garnish
  (optional)

Grease 8-inch springform pan; dust with graham cracker crumbs.
In blender or food processor container spoon cottage cheese.
Process until smooth. Add yogurt, mayonnaise, sugar, lemon peel,
lemon juice and vanilla; process until smooth. Add egg whites;
process until well mixed. Pour into prepared pan. Bake in 325°F
oven 30 minutes. Turn off oven. Leave cheesecake in oven with
door ajar 30 minutes. Cool in pan on wire rack. Cover; chill
several hours. Before serving, remove side of pan. Serve with
Raspberry Sauce. If desired, garnish with fresh raspberries.

Makes 8 servings

Raspberry Sauce: In blender or food processor puree 1
package (10 ounces) frozen raspberries, thawed; strain. Stir in 1/3
cup Karo light or dark corn syrup. Makes about 2 1/2 cups.

Microwave Brownie Cups

1 cup Microwave Brownie &
  Cake Mix (recipe on
  page 84)
1 egg, lightly beaten

1/4 cup HELLMANN'S® or BEST
  FOODS® Real, Light or
  Cholesterol Free Reduced
  Calorie Mayonnaise

Microwave Directions: Line 6 (2 1/2-inch) microwavable muffin pan
cups with paper liners.* In medium bowl combine mix, egg and
mayonnaise; stir until well blended. Spoon into muffin cups.
Microwave on HIGH (100%), turning once, 2 1/2 minutes. Cool in
pan on flat heatproof surface. *Makes 6 brownie cups*

*To make without a microwavable muffin pan, use 2 paper liners
for each brownie. Arrange liners in circular pattern on
microwavable plate. Continue as above.

Light 'n Luscious Cheesecake

Secret Chocolate Sensation

1 package (18¼ or 18½
  ounces) pudding-included
  chocolate cake mix
1 cup water
3 eggs

1 cup HELLMANN'S® or BEST
  FOODS® Real, Light or
  Cholesterol Free Reduced
  Calorie Mayonnaise

Grease and flour 2 (9×1½-inch) round cake pans. In large bowl
with mixer at low speed, beat cake mix, water, eggs and
mayonnaise just until blended. Beat at medium speed 2 minutes.
Pour into prepared pans. Bake in 350°F oven 30 to 35 minutes or
until cake springs back when touched lightly in center. Cool in
pans on wire racks 10 minutes. Remove from pans; cool
completely on racks. Fill and frost as desired.

Makes 1 (9-inch) layer cake

Chocolate Tube Cake: Follow recipe for Secret Chocolate
Sensation. Grease and flour 12-cup fluted tube pan. Pour batter
into prepared pan. Bake in 350°F oven 40 to 45 minutes or until
cake springs back when touched lightly in center. Cool in pan on
wire rack 20 minutes. Remove from pan; cool completely on rack.
Glaze as desired.

Microwave Chocolate Cupcakes

1 cup Microwave Brownie &
  Cake Mix (recipe on
  page 84)
1 egg, lightly beaten
¼ cup milk

¼ cup HELLMANN'S® or BEST
  FOODS® Real, Light or
  Cholesterol Free Reduced
  Calorie Mayonnaise

Microwave Directions: Line 6 (2½-inch) microwavable muffin pan
cups with paper liners.* In medium bowl combine mix, egg, milk
and mayonnaise; stir until well blended. Spoon into muffin cups.
Microwave on HIGH (100%), turning once, 3 minutes. Cupcakes
will appear moist. Cool in pan on flat heatproof surface. Frost if
desired. *Makes 6 cupcakes*

*To make without microwavable muffin pan, use 2 paper liners
for each cupcake. Arrange liners in circular pattern on
microwavable plate. Continue as above. (Cupcakes will spread
slightly.)

California Date-Nut Muffins

Mazola No Stick cooking
  spray
1 cup all-purpose flour
1/3 cup sugar
1/4 cup whole wheat flour
1 1/2 teaspoons baking powder
1/8 teaspoon salt
1 cup chopped pitted dates
1 egg, lightly beaten

1/3 cup HELLMANN'S® or BEST
  FOODS® Real, Light or
  Cholesterol Free Reduced
  Calorie Mayonnaise
1/3 cup water
1/2 teaspoon vanilla
1/2 cup coarsely chopped
  walnuts

Spray 10 (2 1/2-inch) muffin pan cups with cooking spray. In large
bowl combine all-purpose flour, sugar, whole wheat flour, baking
powder and salt. Stir in dates. In small bowl combine egg,
mayonnaise, water and vanilla until smooth. Stir into flour
mixture just until moistened. Spoon into each prepared muffin
pan cup. Sprinkle with chopped walnuts. Bake in 375°F oven 30
minutes or until golden. Immediately remove from pan. Cool on
wire rack or serve warm.   *Makes 10 muffins*

Sunday Morn
Cranberry-Orange Bread

2 cups flour
1 cup fresh or frozen
  cranberries, coarsely
  chopped
3/4 cup sugar
1/2 cup coarsely chopped
  walnuts
2 teaspoons baking powder

1/4 teaspoon salt
1 egg, lightly beaten
1 teaspoon grated orange peel
1/2 cup orange juice
1/3 cup HELLMANN'S® or BEST
  FOODS® Real, Light or
  Cholesterol Free Reduced
  Calorie Mayonnaise

Grease and flour 2 (7 1/2×3 3/4×2 1/4-inch) loaf pans. In large bowl
combine flour, cranberries, sugar, walnuts, baking powder and
salt. In small bowl beat egg, orange peel, orange juice and
mayonnaise until smooth; stir into flour mixture just until
moistened. Spoon into prepared pans. Bake in 350°F oven 60 to
70 minutes or until toothpick inserted into center comes out
clean. Cool in pans on wire racks 10 minutes. Remove from pans;
cool completely on racks.   *Makes 2 loaves*

Note: Bread is easier to slice on second day.

Scrumptious Carrot Cake

1 package (18¼ to 18½
    ounces) pudding-included
    yellow cake mix
2 teaspoons cinnamon
½ teaspoon nutmeg
½ teaspoon ground ginger
¾ cup HELLMANN'S® or BEST
    FOODS® Real, Light or
    Cholesterol Free Reduced
    Calorie Mayonnaise
3 eggs

2 cups coarsely shredded
    carrots
1 can (8 ounces) crushed
    pineapple, well drained
1 cup coarsely chopped
    walnuts
    Cream Cheese Frosting
    (recipe follows)
    Chopped walnuts and
    shredded carrot for
    garnish (optional)

Grease and flour 13×9×2-inch baking pan. In large bowl with mixer at low speed, beat cake mix, cinnamon, nutmeg and ginger until blended. Add mayonnaise, eggs, carrots and pineapple. Beat 30 seconds or until moistened. Reduce speed to medium; beat 2 minutes. Stir in nuts. Pour into prepared pan. Bake in 350°F oven 30 to 35 minutes or until cake springs back when touched lightly in center. Cool in pan on wire rack. Frost with Cream Cheese Frosting. If desired, garnish with chopped walnuts and shredded carrot. *Makes 12 servings*

Cream Cheese Frosting: In medium bowl combine 1 package (3 ounces) softened cream cheese, 2 cups powdered sugar, 2 tablespoons softened Mazola margarine or butter, 2 teaspoons lemon juice and 1 teaspoon vanilla. Beat until smooth.

Scrumptious Carrot Cake

Microwave Chocolate Cake

Mazola No Stick cooking
  spray
2 cups Microwave Brownie &
  Cake Mix (recipe on
  page 84)
2 eggs, lightly beaten

$^1/_2$ cup HELLMANN'S® or BEST
  FOODS® Real, Light or
  Cholesterol Free Reduced
  Calorie Mayonnaise
$^1/_2$ cup milk

Microwave Directions: Spray 9-inch round microwavable cake pan
with cooking spray. In medium bowl combine mix, eggs,
mayonnaise and milk; stir until well blended. Pour into prepared
cake pan. Microwave on MEDIUM (50%), turning once, 7 minutes.
Turn pan; microwave on HIGH (100%) 3 minutes longer or until
toothpick inserted 1 inch from edge comes out clean. Cool in
pan on flat heatproof surface. Frost if desired.

Makes 1 (9-inch) cake

Chili-Cheese Corn Muffins

Mazola No Stick cooking
  spray
1 cup yellow corn meal
$^3/_4$ cup flour
2 tablespoons sugar
1 tablespoon baking powder
$^1/_4$ teaspoon salt
1 egg, lightly beaten
$^2/_3$ cup milk
$^1/_3$ cup HELLMANN'S® or BEST
  FOODS® Real, Light or
  Cholesterol Free Reduced
  Calorie Mayonnaise

1 can (7 ounces) corn *or* corn
  with green and red sweet
  peppers, drained
$^1/_2$ cup (2 ounces) shredded
  Cheddar cheese
3 to 6 tablespoons chopped
  green chilies, undrained

Spray 12 (2$^1/_2$-inch) muffin pan cups with cooking spray. In large
bowl combine corn meal, flour, sugar, baking powder and salt. In
small bowl combine egg, milk and mayonnaise; stir in corn,
cheese and chilies until well mixed. Stir corn mixture into flour
mixture just until moistened. Spoon into each prepared muffin
pan cup. Bake in 400°F oven 20 to 25 minutes or until golden.
Immediately remove from pan. Serve warm.

Makes 12 muffins

Cheddar-Onion Casserole Bread

2 1/2 cups flour
  1 tablespoon baking powder
  1/2 teaspoon salt
  1/2 cup HELLMANN'S® or BEST
    FOODS® Real, Light or
    Cholesterol Free Reduced
    Calorie Mayonnaise

2 cups (8 ounces) shredded
    Cheddar cheese
  1/2 cup minced green onions
  1 egg
  3/4 cup milk

Grease 1 1/2-quart casserole. In large bowl combine flour, baking powder and salt. Stir in mayonnaise until mixture resembles coarse crumbs. Add cheese and green onions; toss. In small bowl beat egg and milk. Stir into cheese mixture just until moistened. Spoon into prepared casserole. Bake in 425°F oven 35 to 45 minutes or until toothpick inserted into center comes out clean. Cut into wedges; serve immediately.   *Makes 1 loaf*

Bittersweet Brownies

Mazola No Stick cooking
    spray
  4 squares (1 ounce each)
    unsweetened chocolate,
    melted
  1 cup sugar
  1/2 cup HELLMANN'S® or BEST
    FOODS® Real, Light or
    Cholesterol Free Reduced
    Calorie Mayonnaise

2 eggs
  1 teaspoon vanilla
  3/4 cup flour
  1/2 teaspoon baking powder
  1/4 teaspoon salt
  1/2 cup chopped walnuts

Spray 8×8×2-inch baking pan with cooking spray. In large bowl stir chocolate, sugar, mayonnaise, eggs and vanilla until smooth. Stir in flour, baking powder and salt until well blended. Stir in walnuts. Spread evenly in prepared pan. Bake in 350°F oven 25 to 30 minutes or until toothpick inserted into center comes out clean. Cool in pan on wire rack. Cut into 2-inch squares.

Makes 16 brownies

INDEX